PRAISE FOR MALCOLM McDONALD ON ACCOUNT MANAGEMENT

'Following a systematic approach that combines real-world insights with scholarly research, this book is the go-to resource on key account management.' **Professor Mark Johnston, Rollins College, USA, and co-author of the most widely cited sales textbooks in the world**

'Soundly based on accepted theory, this book is an inestimable practical guide to key account management. As a rare collection of wisdom and insight into KAM, it has great value for practitioners and students and is highly recommended for those aiming for the AKAM Diploma. Malcolm McDonald and Beth Rogers were among the very first in the UK to acknowledge and research KAM, making important contributions to this professional discipline that is still poorly understood by most companies.' **Dr Diana Woodburn, Chairman of The Association for Key Account Management**

'This book is an up-to-date and comprehensive piece of knowledge on key account management. The solid frameworks and practical insights it contains, together with the expertise and passion of the authors, offer the reader an engaging learning tool for successful KAM.' **Dr Rodrigo Guesalaga, Director of the KAM Best Practice Research Club, Cranfield University**

'I found this book to be integrating and interesting as it offers some new insights into key account management. It is a must-read for anyone who is working as a key account manager or who is planning to introduce KAM into their organization.' **Dr Kenneth Le Meunier-FitzHugh, Senior Lecturer in Marketing, University of East Anglia**

'Key account management has become increasingly critical to business success. A great combination of key account theory and practice, this book is a must-read for all business leaders.' **Nick Porter, Chairman of the Association of Professional Sales**

Malcolm McDonald on Key Account Management

Malcolm McDonald
with Beth Rogers

First published in Great Britain and the United States in 2017 by Kogan Page Limited

2nd Floor, 45 Gee Street
London
EC1V 3RS
United Kingdom

c/o Martin P Hill Consulting
122 W 27th St, 10th Floor
New York, NY 10001
USA

4737/23 Ansari Road
Daryaganj
New Delhi 110002
India

www.koganpage.com

ISBN   978 0 7494 8077 6
E-ISBN 978 0 7494 8079 0

British Library Cataloguing-in-Publication Data

A CIP record for this book is available from the British Library.

Library of Congress Cataloging-in-Publication Data

Names: McDonald, Malcolm, author. | Rogers, Beth, 1957- author.
Title: Malcolm McDonald on key account management / Malcolm McDonald, Beth
  Rogers.
Description: New York : Kogan Page Ltd, [2017] | Includes bibliographical
  references and index.
Identifiers: LCCN 2017022502 (print) | LCCN 2017030249 (ebook) | ISBN
  9780749480790 (ebook) | ISBN 9780749480776 (alk. paper)
Subjects: LCSH: Marketing--Key accounts. | Selling--Key accounts.
Classification: LCC HF5415.123 (ebook) | LCC HF5415.123 .M33 2017 (print) |
  DDC 658.8/102--dc23

Typeset by Integra Software Services, Pondicherry
Print production managed by Jellyfish
Printed and bound by CPI Group (UK) Ltd, Croydon, CR0 4YY

CONTENTS

ABOUT THE AUTHORS

This book is written by two authors with a passion for helping organizations to grow. We have spent over 20 years researching, teaching and consulting on key account management.

Professor Malcolm McDonald MA (Oxon), MSc, PhD, DLitt, DSc

Malcolm is Emeritus Professor at Cranfield University School of Management, as well as being an honorary professor at Warwick Business School.

Malcolm is a graduate in English Language and Literature from University of Oxford, in Business Studies from Bradford University Management Centre, and has a PhD from Cranfield University. He has written over 40 books, including the bestseller *Marketing Plans: How to prepare them, how to use them*, and more than 100 articles and papers.

Coming from a background in business, which included a number of years as Marketing Director of Canada Dry, Malcolm has successfully maintained a close link between academic rigour and commercial application. He has been a consultant to many major companies from the UK, Europe, the United States, the Far East, South-East Asia, Australasia and Africa, in the areas of strategic marketing and marketing planning, market segmentation, key account management, international marketing and marketing accountability.

Malcolm is Chairman of Malcolm McDonald Consulting Ltd and works with the operating boards of a number of the world's leading multinationals.

Beth Rogers BA, MBA, PhD, PFHEA

Beth Rogers was recently Head of the Marketing and Sales Subject Group at University of Portsmouth Business School. She is best known for pioneering sales education in higher education in the UK. Portsmouth was the first and is still one of the few universities in the UK to be recognized as a 'top sales school' by the global Sales Education Foundation. She is a visiting fellow at Cranfield University School of Management.

Beth's first degree was in Politics with International Studies (Warwick) and she has an MBA from Cranfield. Her doctorate dissertation was on resource decision-making in the sales function. She is a principal fellow of the Higher Education Academy, recognizing not just her reputation in her field, but her achievements in innovative learning and teaching methods and leadership of academic teams. She has authored articles (for academic journals, practitioner magazines and blogs) and four business books, including the popular *Rethinking Sales Management*.

Before her academic career Beth worked in business development roles in the information technology sector and was for nine years a consultant working with global companies across four continents and in a variety of business sectors. She is currently the non-executive director of a small and a medium-sized enterprise.

ABOUT THE CONTRIBUTORS

A book about business challenges needs to be rooted in the experience of people who are making things happen in organizations, day in and day out. We are extremely grateful to the following contributors for sharing their expertise and experience to illustrate points made in this book:

- First of all, a special thank you to Bev Burgess for her guest chapter on account-based marketing. Bev is Senior Vice-President of ITSMA Europe, and leads ITSMA's global Account-Based Marketing (ABM) practice. ITSMA (Information Technology Services Marketing Association) was established over 20 years ago to lead the way in defining, building and inspiring business-to-business (B2B) services marketing excellence.

- Secondly, to our colleague Edmund Bradford, Managing Director of Market2Win Ltd, who has provided an appendix to our key account planning chapter explaining how simulation software can be used in planning and training. Ed produces simulation games to teach students and executives about sales and market strategy. These games are used in several universities on MBA, master's and undergraduate courses.

Our deep-felt thanks are also due to:

- Paul Beaumont, Interim Sales Director, for his contributions and particularly for sanity-checking our first draft.
- Phill McGowan, Chief Executive Officer of Positive Sales Limited, for his contribution and particularly for sanity-checking our second draft.

Our narrative has come alive thanks to the observations of practitioners and we are very grateful to:

- Simon Derbyshire, Vice-President of Capgemini Saudi Arabia.
  Capgemini is a global leader in consulting, technology and outsourcing services.

- Karen Bell, Business Development Director at Ashfield, part of UDG Healthcare plc.
  Ashfield, part of UDG Healthcare plc, is a global leader in commercialization services for the pharmaceutical and healthcare industry.

- Darren Bayley, Commercial Director of Dentsply Sirona
  Dentsply Sirona is the world's largest manufacturer of dental products and technologies.

- Bernard Quancard, President and Chief Executive Officer, Strategic Account Management Association (SAMA).
  SAMA is a unique non-profit association with more than 10,000 members worldwide. SAMA focuses solely on helping establish strategic, key and global account management as a separate profession, career path and proven corporate strategy for growth.

- Rob Maguire, Procurement Consultant and Partner of MaguireIzatt LLP (www.maguireizatt.co.uk).
  MaguireIzatt LLP delivers strategic consultancy services for organizations needing to improve their commercial relationships with their suppliers.

- Duncan Affleck, Global Sales and Business Development Manager, Beran Instruments Ltd.
  Beran Instruments Ltd is a UK-based manufacturer of condition monitoring systems for industrial and utility sectors supplying to the global market.

- Andy Proctor, Innovation Lead, InnovateUK.
  Innovate UK is the UK's innovation agency.

- Cédric Belliard, Field Marketing Manager for a global technology company.

- Mark Jackson, Sales Director, Jackson, Jackson & Sons Ltd.
  Jackson, Jackson & Sons Limited is a leading commercial building contractor in the north-west of England.

- Liz Machtynger, Partner, Customer Essential.
  Customer Essential is a consultancy dedicated to delivering customer management solutions.

- Stuart Moran, Head of Sales – Vertical Markets for a global manufacturing and services company.
- David Lucas-Smith, Enterprise Sales Director for a NASDAQ 100 technology company.
- Steve Jackson, Business Development Manager for a global manufacturing and services company.

ABOUT THIS BOOK

This book explores the challenge of winning, retaining and developing key accounts. It is applicable where businesses sell to businesses, but the principles can also be applied to selling complex products and services to high-net-worth individuals. Key accounts are customers who are important enough to their suppliers to be treated as a market in their own right. Consequently, they wield significant power. Although market share and revenue growth can be achieved, the costs to serve key accounts can erode profitability unless they are thoroughly understood and managed.

Key account management is also known as strategic account management for a good reason. It is a strategic capability. It is about the selection of opportunities and the allocation of scarce resources to those opportunities. It is certainly not easy, and we are very familiar with research showing that commitment is required over a number of years to make sure that key account management programmes evolve and deliver benefits. Making your company attractive to key accounts and adapting to their needs requires analysis, planning, implementation and regular renewal. Change is constant. This book takes a step-by-step approach to presenting best practice, underpinned by objective research sources. Whether your business is starting up or well established, there is always more to discover about improving the way that value is created between you and your most important customers.

This book is written by two authors with a passion for helping companies to grow. We have spent over 20 years researching, teaching and consulting on key account management. We have condensed this knowledge into this book, focusing on making it easy to read and easy to use.

A note about the illustrative case studies

In most chapters in this book, we start by discussing an illustrative case study. These cases are fictional, but designed to illustrate real issues in the field of key account management that we have encountered in our research.

ACKNOWLEDGEMENTS

We dedicate this book to our students on courses and executive education at Cranfield University School of Management and University of Portsmouth Business School, whose diligent interest in our topic has kept us in productive work and has sustained our commitment to creating and sharing knowledge about key account management. We are proud of our alumni, several of whom have made direct and indirect contributions to this book.

We also salute our co-researchers and prior co-authors, especially Tony Millman, Diana Woodburn and Lynette Ryals.

We thank the staff at Kogan Page for their faith in this book and this series, and all their help in producing it.

Introducing key account management

People often ask us why we have devoted so much time to thinking about key account management. We do so because we know that key account management matters. Companies live or die by their key accounts, and that affects the prosperity of all of us.

> Our key accounts are strategically important to us. They provide stability and continuity in our revenue stream. We work to achieve long-term relationships with the key people in the buying teams of key accounts. To support key accounts we have a range of people, all engaged at various levels and across departments – from sales, finance, quality assurance, engineering and customer support. The level of engagement is important to both companies. Both are aware of the need to work together, with the respective account managers and purchasing decision-makers appreciating the need for honest approaches. The key accounts realize that it is important to plan and implement regular supply and payment schedules with us – so that we can continuously provide the level of support that they require. There is an ongoing learning process for both companies in identifying and realizing mutual benefits.
>
> Duncan Affleck, Global Sales and Business Development
> Manager, Beran Instruments Ltd
> *Beran Instruments Ltd is a UK-based manufacturer of condition monitoring systems for industrial and utility sectors supplying to the global market*

If you are working in any business selling to businesses or other complex organizations then you probably have some big, powerful customers that you call key accounts. If you are in a small business, they might even be other small businesses. Some of the principles of key account management also apply in some business-to-consumer (B2C) scenarios such as selling to high-net-worth individuals. You want to succeed with these customers. You want them to appreciate your brand values, the extra service that you give them to help them to achieve their objectives, and you expect that in return they will help you to grow and to achieve your objectives. This is all fine in principle, but never, ever easy. We hope this book will enable you to learn something about the knowledge that is out there about managing key customers, and help you to reflect on your own situations and do things to improve them.

It's not enough these days to service your accounts well with a great portfolio of products and services; customers demand more. Increasingly, your most valued key accounts seek supplier innovation and experienced account managers with new insights that will impact their bottom line. It's time for key account management to up its game. This book is full of useful updates and pragmatic suggestions to do just that.

Sales Director, manufacturing sector

Definitions

What is key account management? We define it as an approach to strategic customers (whose needs you understand in depth), which offers them value that distinguishes you from your competitors.

Who or what are strategic customers? Well, that depends on your company objectives.

The essence of key account management (KAM) is to devote scarce business resources to selected customers, so having too many makes it impossible to serve them all effectively. An analogy can be drawn from our personal lives. Each of us has hundreds of acquaintances, but we have the capacity to love and cherish only a few special friends. The pyramid idea (shown in Figure 1.1), although it is a fairly simplistic illustration, starts to give you some idea of a realistic proportion of key accounts to non-key accounts.

Figure 1.1 Key account preliminary selection

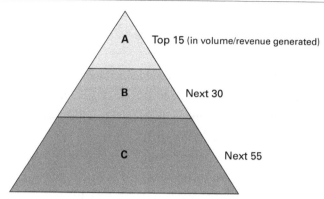

A — Top 15 (in volume/revenue generated)

B — Next 30

C — Next 55

SOURCE adapted from M McDonald teaching material, Cranfield School of Management

Many companies fall into the trap of including too many major customers in their KAM programme, or failing to monitor how the quality of business-to-business (B2B) relationships change over time – with some key accounts dropping to non-key status, and new key accounts emerging from other customer segments. We will discuss the dynamic nature of business relationships throughout this book.

KAM has been a vital capability in companies for over 20 years. Those who do it well have differentiated themselves and enjoyed profitable growth. In spite of this, the strategies necessary to manage major accounts are rarely researched or taught to young people joining the workforce. Equally, ongoing training and development is rarely available to business development professionals who have been working hard to keep up with the speed and complexity of demand in the modern supply chain. As practitioner academics who have spent 20 years trying to address this knowledge gap, we have written this book as an introduction to the strategy and operations of KAM.

The essence of key account management (KAM) is to devote scarce business resources to selected customers, so having too many makes it impossible to serve them all effectively. An analogy can be drawn from our personal lives. Each of us has hundreds of acquaintances, but we have the capacity to love and cherish only a few special friends.

The learning journey in this book

The underlying assumption behind this book is that you have bought it because you want your company or employer to make money – and that if you are already making money you want to make even more. Chapter 2 discusses how key account management (also known as strategic account management) is positioned in the company's overall efforts to generate shareholder value.

Any fool can deliver sales revenue by discounting heavily on big deals. But what is the point of that if not much profit is made out of a contract when all the expenses of serving that customer are taken into account? Professionals in marketing, selling and business development (or however your company describes the function or functions responsible for revenue generation) have a responsibility to add value for shareholders. Primarily they do this by creating highly satisfied customers, but they must also understand the cost base of the company, the cost of capital and the importance of cash flow.

Having made this fundamental point, however, there is a problem, which we will cover in Chapter 3, which discusses customer portfolio analysis and the selection of key accounts. Within overall company performance, there will be some products and some customers that do not make a profit, while others are very profitable. The temptation of some accountants is either to get rid of the loss-making products and customers, or to raise prices in order to make them profitable, thus running the risk of losing them.

Business development managers need to challenge this logic. In the case of Canada Dry, we were expected to carry a full range of soft drinks to meet the needs of customers who wanted to trade with us. The problem was that whilst we specialized in high-quality mixers (soft drinks that are mixed with spirits such as gin and whisky) and made big margins on these, on products such as lemonade we made little, if any, margin. In order to trade, however, we had to have a full range, and without the low-margin products we would not have been able to sell the high-margin products, as customers demanded a full line of soft drinks from their suppliers. It is the same with customers. Sometimes you need a customer on your books who is not very profitable, as long as their role in the customer portfolio contributes towards overall shareholder value.

Ask any director of any company what the biggest challenges are and the answer will always include something about how to deal profitably with big, powerful customers. There are only a few major car companies in the world; most fast-moving consumer goods are sold through a few large retailers in the category – and so on. It would be a huge constraint not to deal with major players in an industry sector, so we have to learn how to be successful in working with them while balancing our risks across the wider customer portfolio.

Why are these customers so powerful? In Chapter 4, we invite readers to put themselves in the shoes of the purchasing professionals of the 21st century. Arguably, the business world in the 1950s and 1960s was fairly complacent. Markets had been growing, and it is easy to succeed where there is growth. The 1970s brought the shock of the oil crisis and the growth of information technology. By the mid-1980s, the globalization of business offered purchasing professionals a whole new world of potential sources of supply, and opportunities to dramatically reduce their employer's cost base. Obviously, they had to manage supply risk as well. As their skills developed to take the new strategic role for purchasing, they needed suppliers who could come on the journey with them. Procurement has continued to gain strategic focus through the recession of the early 1990s, 2000s and the financial crash of 2008. And it is also during difficult economic times that KAM has a strategic advantage – the ability to keep major customers makes a difference to companies' ability to survive recessions.

It was a common mistake among sales practitioners to see the demand for strategic proposals as some kind of icing to put on selling. In fact, purchasing decision-makers were demanding a change from the opportunistic selling of the growth decades. They wanted to discuss their needs with professionals who thoroughly understood their finances, their processes, their organization and their culture. Equally, they wanted suppliers who could offer them boundary-changing solutions, not just products. So in Chapter 4 we explain how purchasing professionals evaluate purchase categories and suppliers. Walk a while in their shoes and imagine how they see you as a supplier compared to your competitors. It can be uncomfortable, but it is absolutely necessary.

In Chapter 5 we discuss how to analyse the needs of key accounts and develop meaningful value propositions. It includes a lot of tables, charts and analyses that you might find useful in building your own key account plan. The extent of analysis we recommend for key accounts will underline our assertion that most companies do not really have a lot of key accounts. Key account planning can take a lot of time and resource. However, what we want to avoid is readers failing to put enough resource into proposals to key accounts and thus losing business. We have seen the research (that just reinforces common sense): it is better to somewhat over-resource strategic business opportunities than to under-resource them. These planning techniques will help you to assess those resource needs. In Chapter 5 we have also included an appendix written by our colleague Ed Bradford of Market2Win about simulation games that help you to play out key account plans and competitor reactions.

Having mentioned in Chapter 3 the importance of a balanced customer portfolio, we would not want to move on without explaining how technology can help with managing key accounts and with accounts in other positions in your customer portfolio. We are very grateful to Bev Burgess, Senior Vice-President of the Information Technology Services Marketing Association (ITSMA) for her guest chapter (Chapter 6) on account-based marketing (ABM). Technology enables more and more information to be converted into customized proposals and communications to ever more customers. Investments in the latest best practice in IT-driven business development must be made carefully and this chapter should help you to consider the potential of ABM and what it may have to offer your organization. There are case studies in the appendices to this chapter.

Resourcing challenges and solutions are explored in Chapter 7. If KAM requires a deep understanding of the business of major customers, this requires professional key account managers, and may also require ad hoc or even semi-permanent teams of people with different functional skills or knowledge to design value propositions. This is a considerable investment, which needs to be carefully managed. One of the quickest ways to go bankrupt is to 'delight' all your customers; Chapter 7 also considers alternative resourcing models for other customer segments. The principles of classifying customers according to their potential for profitable growth over time, offset by your competitive strengths in meeting their needs, must lead to differential resource allocation. Such a classification would lead to the correct setting of objectives and allocation of scarce resources. It is not feasible to over-service every customer segment.

Business is global, and globalization underpinned the transition from purchasing to strategic sourcing. Just as purchasers demand strategic value propositions, they expect suppliers to be able to deliver them across the globe. Chapter 8 demonstrates models for internationalization and explains some factors that can help companies to internationalize with their key accounts – and some things that inhibit internationalization. In particular, we discuss working across very different cultures. Once again, we offer analysis tools that can help you to decide what best suits your company.

Key account management is also known as strategic account management for good reason. It is a strategic capability. It is about the selection of opportunities and the allocation of scarce resources to those opportunities. It is certainly not easy, and we are very familiar with research showing that commitment is required over a number of years to make sure that KAM programmes evolve and deliver benefits. In Chapter 9, we cover implementation issues, reviews and risk management.

Finally, we gaze into our crystal ball, and invite our practitioner contributors to gaze into their crystal balls, and we look forward to the future of KAM. We feel quite confident about doing this. When we wrote about KAM 20 years ago we did the same, and our reflection in the appendix to Chapter 10 suggests we did call quite a few things quite well. We know that, as business practitioners, you need to know not just what accumulated best practice tells us about today, but whether it will tell us anything useful for the future.

Overall, this book is designed to equip readers with ideas about how to manage their own key accounts. Drafts have been reviewed by practitioners, and key account managers, sales directors, entrepreneurs and purchasing professionals have kindly offered their observations to help to illustrate points made. No two implementations of KAM can be the same, but we feel that the core techniques presented in this book will provide the raw materials for wherever you want to go with your KAM programme. Now let's start at the beginning – how KAM sits within the business and helps it to sustain profitable growth...

Action list

Reflect on what your organization is trying to achieve.

Can you identify what it is that makes your key accounts key to the business?

Is there alignment between key account activity and business objectives?

We will consider these items further in Chapter 2.

The role of key accounts in achieving business growth 02

This chapter discusses how key accounts can help your company to grow. In addition to introducing a method of analysing and mapping business growth strategies, it includes latest thinking about the relative positioning of key account management (KAM) with other types of customer. Briefly, we introduce the role of technology in enhancing customer relationships, a hot topic that is revisited in depth in Chapter 6. We also explain how planning for key accounts needs to align with marketing plans and corporate plans.

We begin this chapter with a very short case study based on a real example. We will refer to the case study later in the chapter, and at the end of the chapter we present a solution.

CASE STUDY TIX Solutions Ltd

TIX is a medium-sized provider of information technology systems, a value-added reseller (VAR) for some big names in hardware. They provided a major systems upgrade for a government department five years ago. The department relocated to a town five years ago to generate new jobs in a deprived area. TIX was chosen as a supplier because of its local roots, and the contract helped the company to grow. The agreement included maintenance, training and a service-level agreement for user support.

The board of TIX and the senior civil servants have cordial meetings, but the key account manager is dealing with a great deal of unrest from the technical staff and users of the system. The system should have already been upgraded, but budget costs have meant that it has been delayed. The best that the TIX engineers can do is replace components as they fail, but that is affecting availability of the system. Security has also moved on in the last five years, which means that TIX software analysts have to apply a lot of temporary fixes to ensure data protection. The key account manager is concerned that TIX will be blamed for problems arising from the customer's inability to invest. Meanwhile, when all the labour costs are applied to the contract, it is looking like the profitability of this customer relationship is weak.

So, it is a mixed blessing when a new government minister does agree to fund investment. However, during the budget negotiation it has been decided that the department will contract out all information technology functions as a managed service. The contract duration is 10 years. The new service must include the implementation of a new communications technology, which should save a great deal of government money. Proposals will be sought worldwide, and purchasing consultants will handle the bidding process.

This opportunity poses a number of strategic questions for TIX. TIX can offer a managed service, but the company is by no means a market leader in managed services. Since so little was known about the government minister's announcement in advance, the key account manager feels sure that a competitor influenced the new plan. Also, if TIX bids for this, it will have to take on the customer staff who have been unhappy with the company. They will be difficult to manage. TIX will have to implement a new technology that they know, but regard as still having many flaws. Nevertheless, it seems unthinkable that TIX should lose this flagship customer. If a competitor wins, they are highly likely to poach key TIX personnel.

TIX senior managers need to refer to the overall strategic plan. How much should be invested in selling a bigger service offering to an existing customer? Is the new technology an opportunity or a threat? Will they have to partner with a bigger player to make a proposal? What would losing a big but barely profitable customer do to the business?

Key accounts can make or break a business. When we are doing all the right things for them, the relationship is positive and our mutual revenues grow. When things run out of steam, or there are new directions in either company, or new people, things get difficult and brave decisions are needed. TIX had a great key account that was helping them to achieve their business objectives, now they have a potential crisis. In order to appreciate the role of key accounts in achieving business objectives, let's take a look at the way that business objectives and strategies are created.

Developing strategies for profitable growth

KAM can be an integral part of profitable growth. About 200 rigorous academic studies of KAM practices have been published in the last 30 years, and the vast majority report significant relational and financial benefits for the suppliers who implement KAM effectively. However, the evidence is not unanimous. Problems can occur in key accounts, and it is essential for companies to monitor the contribution that key accounts are making to profit and growth. In some cases, the benefit of key accounts can be the scope that they provide or reducing risk in some operations. Profit can be indirect as well as direct.

In this chapter, we focus first on the business objective of growth. Growth in all economies comes from smaller companies getting bigger. Big companies have less room to grow, but they are always up for taking a slice of market share from competitors. So, we can assume that a strategy such as KAM is going to be focused on growing the business overall. Indeed, many small businesses grow by working with bigger key accounts.

Let's start with some core definitions. Objectives are *what* you want to achieve; strategies are *how* you are going to achieve them. Although we are not in an adversarial struggle with customers, it is useful to adopt a military analogy to distinguish strategy from tactics in marketing and sales planning. In military conflict, strategy is the conduct of the war and tactics are the conduct of the battle. So, if you have an objective to grow sales by 10 per cent over three years, of which 7 per cent will be delivered by your KAM strategy, working with key account X on a new formula for their Y product would be a tactic.

Key account management (KAM) can be an integral part of profitable growth. About 200 rigorous academic studies of KAM practices have been published in the last 30 years, and the vast majority report significant relational and financial benefits for the suppliers who implement KAM effectively.

Markets and products in business strategy

Many readers will be familiar with Michael Porter's generic strategies of cost leadership, differentiation and niche, but a more actionable approach to business strategy that resonates well with marketing and sales professionals was devised by another great thinker – Igor Ansoff. His approach to business strategy is shown in Figure 2.1.

Figure 2.1   Ansoff matrix

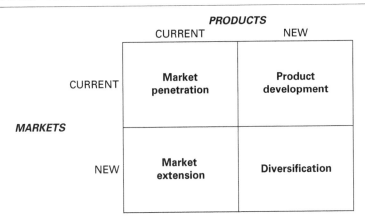

SOURCE adapted from Ansoff (1957)

Ansoff's analysis advises four categories of strategic activity in organizations focused on growth. Selling current products to current customers (market penetration) and developing new products for current customers (product development) are highly relevant to KAM. The TIX case has elements of this. Selling current products to new customers (market extension) is relevant to overall marketing and sales management, as new key accounts will be needed over time. Selling new products to new customers (diversification) is generally regarded as high risk.

Not all strategic directions are equal in importance or desirability. One well-known multinational organization has argued that in sales effort alone, the top-left box requires 1 unit of sales effort, the top-right box requires 4 units of sales effort, the bottom-left box requires 40 units of sales effort, whilst the bottom-right box (new products to new markets) requires 400 units of sales effort!

The main box of interest in most businesses is the top-left box – your current products that you sell to your current markets/customers. Your current strategic customers, usually called 'key accounts', sit in this box. Within each of those key accounts you need separate plans for how you are going to improve productivity and grow share of the account's spend. We discuss this further in Chapter 5. For now, we want you to think carefully about the overall goals for the business.

How strategies contribute to the achievement of objectives

When planning ahead, the first thing a businessperson does is set a MUST goal to achieve in, say, three years' time. For example, one of the authors is the chairman of a company with a £5 million turn-over. He knows that in order to sell the company in three years' time, turnover needs to be £10 million by then, so for him this is the MUST objective. In any endeavour in life, whether it is about success in sports, in managing the home or personal relationships, you need to identify the ideal end-position (the MUST goal). You then review where you are now, and estimate how far away that goal is from the current situation. Then you plan a way forward. Sometimes, the MUST goal is very simply the survival of the business.

As successful senior managers set future goals they also reflect on the past. Where have we come from? How did we get to our current position? What does that tell us about how we can move forward?

Let's take a look at how one enterprising construction company dealt with the 2008 economic crash:

After the financial crash in 2008 many construction companies faced contraction or extinction as new building work stopped and maintenance work was postponed. Those who survived had to do a 'root and branch' review of their businesses. In my business, we decided to implement KAM. First of all, it helped us to keep existing customers. In a sector that is usually transactional, we looked after them. More importantly, KAM provided a foundation for us to win new business with large organizations in public services or regulated sectors. We decided to gain an understanding of the needs of housing associations and utility companies. We occasionally did business with them, but we planned to become a preferred supplier to particular customers.

It is a complex process to prove yourself worthy of promotion from occasional supplier to preferred supplier, but the benefit is clear – substantial, profitable growth. We had to make contacts, get advice from the professional purchasers in these target customers and do our homework in order to understand what it took to be a 'framework supplier' to a large organization that has to be cost-sensitive, but where trust, reputation and social responsibility are also important. For example, our commitment to recruiting apprentices from the housing estates maintained by our customers helps us to demonstrate that we share our customers' values.

KAM requires a long-term approach to managing customer profitability. We have to invest time and money to design and deliver successful framework bids and renewal bids, but we have faith in our service and our people, and the investment continues to pay off because our win rate is impressive. When we are selected for a new framework agreement our costs then reduce, as we have secured a significant pipeline of opportunities for a period of a few years until renewal. Of course, we have to demonstrate every day that these key accounts are strategically important to us by ensuring that our services delivered for them and that our communications with them are first class.

Winning this additional business has injected life blood into my company and I intend to continue investing in KAM as I move the company into its next stage of growth.

Mark Jackson, Sales Director,
Jackson, Jackson & Sons Ltd, Rochdale, UK

You can see how the success of Jackson, Jackson & Sons Ltd was almost entirely achieved through doing much more business with existing customers by adopting a KAM approach (labelled 'market penetration' in Ansoff's matrix). However, KAM depends on selecting a few customers for special attention, and there will be other customers to consider. Businesses must review the other elements of the Ansoff matrix, and Figure 2.2 shows how a business might choose several pathways to growth.

Figure 2.2 How a business might choose several pathways to grow

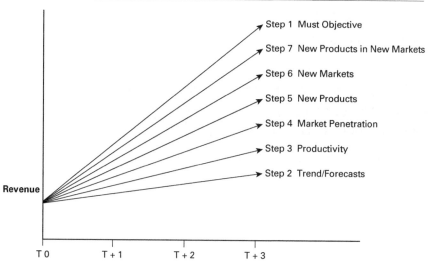

Revenue

Step 1 Must Objective
Step 7 New Products in New Markets
Step 6 New Markets
Step 5 New Products
Step 4 Market Penetration
Step 3 Productivity
Step 2 Trend/Forecasts

T 0   T + 1   T + 2   T + 3

SOURCE adapted from McDonald and Wilson (2011)

In the example shown in Figure 2.2, the MUST goal is revenue-based, and the amount of revenue can be noted on the left-hand vertical axis. On the horizontal axis, you can map the time frame of the plan. T0 means today, T+1 is now plus one year, and so on.

The first step in using this diagram to map your business objectives is to identify the desired revenue in three years' time (the MUST goal). The second step is to enter the revenue figure you are likely to achieve if you carry on doing what you do now. This is the 'trend' line. You may have a good record of year-on-year growth, but trends can go down as well as up.

For the third step, you need to concentrate on the 'productivity' line. We have listed below a number of operational productivity improvements that you should consider for growing your business. For example, we succeeded in gaining a 35 per cent revenue growth in one company by a combination of the following:

- improved product mix;
- improved customer mix;
- smarter sales calls;
- better-targeted promotional activity;

- market-based pricing, including avoidance of discounting;
- delivery charges;
- reduced debtor days.

For the fourth step, we need to consider strategic responses to Ansoff's category 'market penetration' – selling more current products/service to current customers. The example of Jackson, Jackson & Sons Ltd gives us some ideas what these might be:

- understand customers buying needs in depth;
- make a specific offer;
- clearly differentiate your product, service, values and way of doing business.

In other words, KAM. There is much more about how you map your value to customers' needs in Chapter 5.

For the fifth step, consider introducing 'new' products to your existing markets and customers. However, never assume that they will automatically embrace your new ideas. We have seen many key account plans where it has been assumed that as soon as new technology rolls into production, customers will adopt it. They do not. New products can cause disruption and change, which are not welcome. For example, new packaging formats will not be adopted if they do not fit in with massive sunk investments in warehouse design and supermarket shelving. Involve key accounts in new product development from the very early stages. TIX is in a fortunate position in that its customer *wants* new technology, and that is a positive signal in a challenging scenario.

As successful senior managers set future goals, they also reflect on the past. Where have we come from? How did we get to our current position? What does that tell us about how we can move forward?

In our experience, customers like being a key account because they get better service. This is accomplished in two main ways. The first is that the key account manager and key account team facilitate access to myriad product and service offerings from a complex supplier. The second is that being a key account offers improved access to senior managers.

Of course we want the customer to benefit from better service, but our main reason for investing in key accounts is to increase sales and cross-sell new products into the customer. Equally, we look for willingness to build increasing volume incentives into annual agreements. Key account managers have to meet targets and bonuses.

Steve Jackson, Business Development Manager for a global manufacturing and services company

As Steve Jackson indicates, key accounts are chosen to fulfil two growth objectives – market penetration and product development.

For the sixth step, consider taking current products to new markets. Your current markets may decline over time, and if you wish to grow your business you may need to operate in new customers, new sectors or new geographies.

Step 7 allows for consideration of introducing new products into new markets, ie 'Diversification', as shown in Figure 2.1. The history of management is full of examples of the failure of diversification and the reason is not hard to understand. Any brand reputation that you have will have been hard earned. Taking new products into new sectors where you are not known is going to take a lot of investment. It is not impossible, but it would not be most strategists' first choice.

Now let's cast our minds back to TIX and their situation. TIX will have to introduce an established product and a relatively new product into its government department customer just to keep the business. That will absorb a lot of resources. If the company has an ambitious 'must do' objective, then perhaps a way has to be found to achieve it.

It would certainly be difficult to downsize if they lose this customer. So, how much should they invest in this bigger service offering? A better question might be how much they can engage the customer in sharing some of the risks of the investment, in return for rewards such as rebates when cost savings are realized in the future. As a new technology company, although they are concerned about the flaws in the new software platform that the customer wants, they do need to offer new platforms, so TIX must invest in developing the skills.

One possibility would be to contract some of the business to a partner. Working with third parties and with supply chain networks is quite common in complex business sectors. KAM is not always just a relationship between a supplier and a customer. Although we mostly refer in this book to supplier–customer relationships, some key accounts are channel partners such as resellers, specifiers (such as architects in the construction sector), the dominant brands in a supply chain that determine the parts used by sub-assembly manufacturers or influencers, such as consultants.

To conclude this review of defining your sources of business growth, once you have mapped the strategies necessary to move the business towards its MUST goal, more detailed planning is required. When and where growth happens will have an impact on how the company operates – use of fixed assets and working capital, cash flow, recruitment or retraining and even organizational culture. These implications need to be mapped in consultation with finance, operations and human resources experts. Sales professionals sometimes wonder why, when they bring in a big bit of business, it causes a crisis. Someone in operations has a fit because they will have to work extra shifts to make what they have sold. And then someone in finance has a fit because working extra shifts means overtime and that will erode the profitability of the deal and, if the customer does not pay on time, this could stretch cash flow beyond limits agreed with the bank and then – hey presto – we are all out of business.

You cannot consider marketing, sales or key account strategies in isolation, so you need to see not only what your key account can do for growth, but also what it does to the company's capabilities. It is in the interests of companies to derisk operations and cash flow by having a broad portfolio of customers that can be served in different ways.

> *KAM is not always just a relationship between a supplier and a customer. Some key accounts are channel partners such as resellers, specifiers, the dominant brands in a supply chain that determine the parts used by sub-assembly manufacturers or influencers, such as consultants.*

KAM in the customer portfolio

KAM is not the only marketing and sales strategy that a company needs. Figure 2.3 demonstrates a large and complex customer portfolio in a business-sector company. One axis measures sales potential and the other measures costs to serve.

There has been some polarization over the past 20 years between key accounts and large numbers of smaller or cost-driven customers who are happy to do business over internet portals, or with third-party sales organizations. Key accounts are an important source of revenue and profits for organizations. *However, companies should never overlook the profitability of transactional business or what is often called the 'mid-tier', nor should they overlook the small customers using the portal, as some of them will grow. To fit KAM into the company's overall business strategy, it must always be seen in the context of the full customer portfolio.*

Customers come in many different shapes and sizes. Careful segmentation of the total customer base will ensure appropriate levels of service. Let's consider the categories in Figure 2.3:

Figure 2.3   The customer portfolio

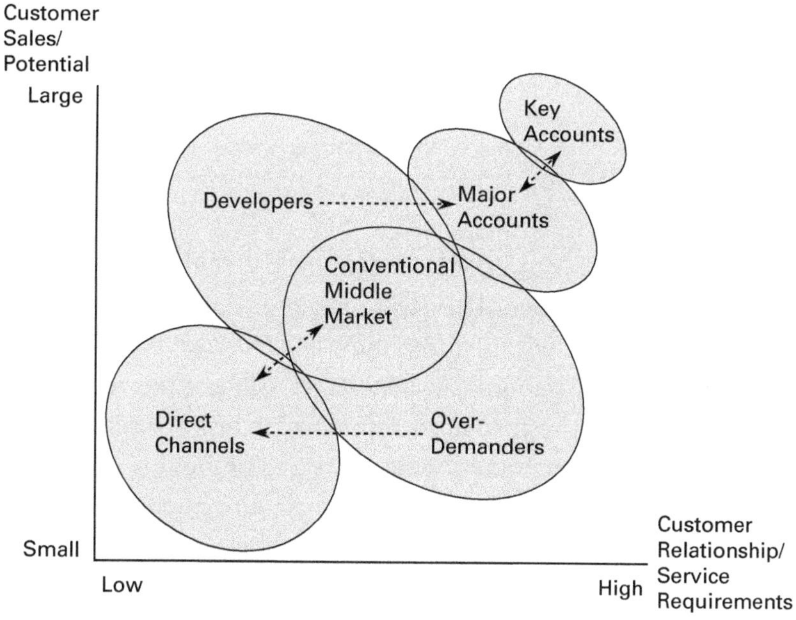

SOURCE adapted from Piercy and Lane (2006)

- Key accounts are few in number. They have huge potential, but it is also complex to serve them.
- Major accounts are either on their way to becoming key accounts or are key accounts in decline.
- The conventional middle market, or mid-tier, is an important part of a customer portfolio and is frequently neglected. It includes future key accounts and, if given focus, it can be very profitable.
- It is noted here that some middle-market accounts develop into major accounts (developers).
- Some middle-market accounts may demand service that is not appropriate to their sales potential (over-demanders).
- Customers with small sales potential and service requirements can easily be served by account-based marketing (ABM) via an online portal, telesales or contract sales organizations. The role of technology in providing customized communications and offers to smaller customers is a 'mega-trend' in business development.

> Specialty chemicals giant Dow Corning caught its competitors by surprise in 2002 when it launched Xiameter, a web-based discount sales channel whose mandate was to bring in new business as well as retain cost-conscious customers who were fleeing their traditional, high-touch relationship with the company.
>
> Loren Gary in *Strategy & Innovation*, 7 March 2005

Loren Gary went on to explain that industry analysts thought that this was a suicidal move. They were wrong. Xiameter paid back its investment to Dow within three months. The key accounts in the cosmetics and telecommunications sectors still got the research and development expertise they needed to develop new formulae for new products; and the customers who wanted commodity products at best prices used the portal. So, KAM can sit alongside other marketing and sales strategies to achieve business objectives.

Some business relationships are simple, as simple as selling tins of beans directly to a corner shop. Some are more complex, involving a myriad of routes of supply to the ultimate user. For example, my business involves supplying electrification, automation and digitalization products to industrial companies. It has an extremely convoluted supply chain involving distributors, value-added resellers, contractors and others.

Do simple transactional business relationships need KAM, however big they are? I think not, I believe this is where account-based marketing (ABM) and e-commerce fits the customer need and saves cost for the supplier.

Where supply is complex, and where relationships are needed throughout the supply chain, especially with specifiers who are not direct customers, a KAM strategy is critical. The relationships with customers and other players in the supply chain need to be high, wide and deep. In other words, there needs to be relationships at board level between the two companies, across the breadth of functions and divisions of both companies and to a considerable degree of detailed mutual understanding. The key account manager has to demonstrate an in-depth knowledge of not only the customer's business, but of the whole sector and supply chain, and has to develop credibility and trust with sophisticated buying professionals so that he/she will be able to advise the customer about preparing for the future. I believe that in complex scenarios the future of the KAM is secure.

ABM still plays a role in key account relationships and can create value for the customer in automating day-to-day transactions and communications. But where idea generation, expert judgement, complex multi-stakeholder, multi-criteria decision-making and multiple-outcome negotiations are concerned – KAM is still king.

Stuart Moran, Head of Sales – Vertical Markets for a global manufacturing, engineering and services company

Key accounts are strategic to companies and, as Stuart Moran suggests, they are not going out of fashion anytime yet. But other parts of the customer portfolio can also deliver profitable growth. The use of technology to provide services to smaller customers and to gather information about their buying behaviour is a key area of investment in many businesses. Perhaps the technology is attractive because it can reduce the costs to serve customers, but it can also provide convenience and choice to customers that they did not have before. It may also be able to generate enough insight about non-key accounts so that the key accounts of the future can be spotted. Is a small company that is constantly exceeding its credit limit a debtor to sue? Not if your system gathers external information about customers and spots that this company is enjoying high growth. Then it is time for a chat about helping them to grow more in return for a bigger share of their business.

The role of technology in managing a customer portfolio

Our contributor Stuart Moran has mentioned ABM as a way to provide good service to less complex customers. ABM is a term often confused with key account management (KAM), but it should be separately defined. ABM involves *integrated marketing and sales communications focused on individual customers or prospects*. It is the opposite of 'spray and pray' marketing, which is particularly wasteful in B2B markets. The advantage of modern customer relationship management (CRM) systems is that much more data can be gathered about customer buying behaviour, so that even occasional buyers on a company portal can receive customized offers relevant to their usage patterns (ABM).

Table 2.1 summarizes the role of ABM in the different types of customers illustrated in Figure 2.3. It is likely that the small accounts using direct channels will receive promotional messages driven by a CRM system, without much intervention from marketing or sales. If the direct channel is an outsourced contract sales organization (perhaps telesales) or sales agent, more intervention is required from marketing, but many organizations share systems with contractors so that they can be prompted by particular buying patterns to respond to the customer. These accounts may move into the mid-market in due course if development activity is successful.

The mid-market or mid-tier accounts probably will have a named account manager, even if it is a desk-based or telephone account manager. Mid-market accounts may also be managed by contract sales organizations so that they can receive focus. Much business with mid-tier accounts can be driven by ABM. However, skill is required to discern the 'developers' who are the key accounts of tomorrow. There may be unprofitable accounts in this section of the customer portfolio ('over-demanders') but there is research to suggest that overall the mid-tier is profitable and may even be a more profitable segment than key accounts.

Major accounts and key accounts normally have a dedicated account manager, but ABM plays a role in ensuring that these accounts are well served by excellent processes and communications. Major accounts are often described as big accounts that are not necessarily strategic. They need to be *kept*, but are not necessarily key.

Table 2.1   The role of account-based marketing across different types of customers

Position in Portfolio	Role of ABM	Staff Support
Key accounts	Operational infrastructure, process excellence, regular communication platform	Key account manager and key account team
Major accounts		Major account manager
Developing mid-market		Business development/ senior sales
Medium sales potential/medium service requirements	Supportive – monitors buying behaviour and drives prompts to customer and telesales team	Telephone account management
Over-demanding mid-market		Telephone account management
Low sales potential/low service requirements	Proactive – monitors buying behaviour and drives direct communications and order prompts to customer	Very limited – such as call handlers

SOURCE adapted from material provided by Paul Beaumont, Interim Sales Director

ABM is a very important trend in B2B marketing and it must be considered alongside KAM. Financial decision-makers will always want to know whether costs to serve a customer can be reduced, and the digitization of marketing and selling activity obviously offers an opportunity for reducing costs to serve and improving the targeting of marketing and sales activity. Further information on ABM and its role in KAM is provided in Chapter 6, which has been written by an industry specialist.

The positioning of KAM in corporate and marketing plans

There are lots of plans that have to come together before a company can go to its shareholders and make a statement about where it is going and why they should invest more. Figure 2.4 shows a hierarchy of plans in a large organization.

Figure 2.4   Hierarchy of plans in a large organization

Corporate Plan								
Marketing Plan								Other functional plans
Key account management overview			Major accounts plan	Plan for mid-tier		Consolidated segment plan		
Key account 1	Key account 2	Key account 3		Mid-tier sector 1	Mid-tier sector 2	Small customers segment 1	Small customers segment 2	

SOURCE adapted from McDonald and Rogers (1998)

Of course, investors are not just impressed by the quality of the planning, and we will now say a few words about 'the bigger picture' that many shareholders expect today, and which has an influence on the way KAM is implemented.

Corporate plans

Figure 2.5 shows some components of a typical corporate plan.

Figure 2.5   Components of a typical corporate plan

> **Corporate objectives and strategies**
>
> • Corporate objectives (what): Profit
> • Corporate Strategies (how):
>> ➤ facilities (ie operations, R and D, IT, distribution etc)
>> ➤ people (personnel)
>> ➤ money (finance)
>> ➤ products and markets (marketing)
>> ➤ other (CSR, image etc)

SOURCE adapted from McDonald and Wilson (2011)

Businesses can have a number of objectives, but care needs to be taken in considering how progress towards them is to be measured. Unless you can measure it, it is not an objective. Hence, expressions such as 'maximize', 'minimize', 'penetrate' and the like are not corporate objectives, because they are not specific enough. Of course, quantifiable objectives represent your destination. Along the journey, the quality of your activities also has to be measured.

We have talked about revenue objectives and business growth, but company valuations also depend on profits. Marketing and sales objectives and strategies should be reviewed in terms of costs to serve the customers, by segment and by key account. What is the most efficient use of cash flow, capital and people per customer to ensure that the company can continue to be successful?

They also need to be evaluated for reputational impact. These days, many companies use the triple bottom line (TBL) technique to rate their performance. Businesses can enhance their brand's reputation by using internal and external measures of environmental, social and economic performance. The 'triple' in bottom line means positive impacts on people, profit and planet. Of course, the core sustainability of the organization is rooted in profit. If a company fails to satisfy its customers' needs better than its competitors and make a profit, employees lose their jobs, charities no longer get their money and local communities no longer benefit from their support.

KAM must be an integral part of the marketing strategy, but it also touches so many other parts of the business. Value for key accounts is achieved through specific operations, technology, logistics, etc. All organizations have scarce resources and these need to be allocated in the most appropriate way in order to achieve the corporate profit objective. KAM objectives and strategies have to be integrated into the corporate plan via the marketing plan. Strategic plans for each key account will have to be amalgamated into an overall picture that explains volumes of business from key accounts and affects the introduction of new product/service offerings. It will also inform how much new business is needed from other parts of the customer portfolio.

Marketing plans

> *The marketing plan should create a pool of possibilities for key account managers looking for ideas to take to key accounts.*

Marketing plans are not just about advertising campaigns. They should provide a rigorous approach to matching company capabilities to customers' needs and planning how value is delivered to the customer, as well as how it is communicated.

Figure 2.6 shows components of a strategic marketing plan.

Figure 2.6   Components of a strategic marketing plan

```
Strategic Marketing Plan

Contents

  • Financial summary
  • Market overview
    o How the market works
    o Key segments and their needs
  • SWOT analysis of segments
  • Portfolio summary of SWOTs
  • Assumption
  • Objectives and strategies
  • Budget
  • Risks and contingencies
```

SOURCE adapted from McDonald and Wilson (2011)

The contents must be rich in actionable ideas in order to create sustainable competitive advantage, that is – creating shareholder value, not just in any one trading period but in a sustainable way over the planning period, which should be at least three years ahead. The marketing plan should create a pool of possibilities for key account managers looking for ideas to take to key accounts.

Figure 2.7 contrasts marketing strategies strongly associated with sustaining competitive advantage with those that are weak.

Without doubt, the main weakness identified by research is companies continuing to define their markets in terms of *products* rather than *needs*.

Figure 2.7 Contrasting marketing strategies

Over 40 years of research into the link between long-run financial success and excellent marketing strategies reveal the following:

Excellent Strategies	Weak Strategies
➤ **Understand markets in depth**	➤ **Always talk about products**
• Target needs-based segments	• Target product categories
• Make a specific offer to each segment	• Make similar offers to all segments
• Have clear differentiation, positioning and branding	• Have no differentiation and poor positioning and branding
• Leverage their strengths and minimize their weaknesses	• Have little understanding of their strengths and weaknesses
• Anticipate the future	• Plan using historical data

SOURCE adapted from M McDonald teaching material, Cranfield School of Management

Understanding customers' needs is widely recognized as the heartbeat of successful marketing. It is also integral to KAM. Table 2.2 illustrates this point.

A company like TIX Solutions Ltd needs to recognize what its customers are trying to achieve. Of course TIX has to understand

Table 2.2 Understanding customers' needs

How customers talk about their IT needs...	
Customer View	**Supplier View**
Give us advice about...	
Cutting costs	PaaS, SaaS, IaaS
Future technology directions	Internet of things: sensors, actuators
Give us help...	
Designing and configuring our systems	Landscape virtualization
Making our processes easier and better	Business optimization analytics
Doing business with our customers electronically	Shopify, Volusion
Take on the burden of...	
Networks managed across international boundaries	WANs, Cloud; meta-networks
Network security	Blockchain framework
Recovering from a flood	Azure, VMware
Making the website mobile-friendly	Git, Sails, Bluemix

SOURCE adapted from M McDonald teaching material, Cranfield School of Management the technology needed to achieve it, but must not assume that the customers will understand the technology or care about it.

Needs analysis in key accounts

What makes it even more challenging in B2B marketing is that different decision-makers in each key account will have different personal and professional needs.

Figure 2.8 shows the results of a study that might help TIX to personify the attitudes of members of the buying team of its key account. On the horizontal axis, attitudes towards a purchase are on a spectrum from the expectation of reward that indicates interest in strategic gain, to relief, which indicates the desire to avoid a

Figure 2.8 Understand the different category buyers

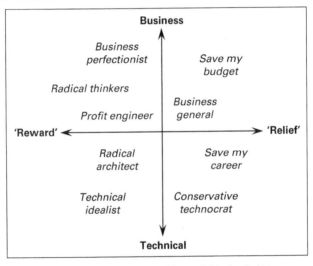

SOURCE adapted from M McDonald teaching material, Cranfield School of Management

problem or operational hassle. On the vertical axis, the attitude of the buying decision-maker is on a spectrum from a business orientation to a technical specialism. So, those who are looking ahead for the business with a reward outlook may be radical strategists looking for big ideas from suppliers, whereas those in the relief/technical quadrant would only be interested in hearing that the supplier can offer something that will save their careers. It is difficult to propose both, but a key account manager would have to understand all these different attitudes and be able to address their needs in the proposed solution.

We expect that marketing managers in companies like TIX are compiling marketing plans that drive the dynamics of the whole customer portfolio, but also ensuring operational support, such as research about decision-makers, for key account managers. Roles and responsibilities between marketing and account managers vary, and we are not blind to the fact that, in many organizations, sales and marketing do not have a happy relationship. There is a growing body of research showing the benefits of sales and marketing integration, but also some that reminds us that there should be creative conflict between these two functions from time to time. In short, marketing should be generating an overall brand preference for a company's generic value proposition, while the key account manager focuses on individual customers, with communications support from marketing, such as customer-specific research and news, case studies, presentation materials and meeting scenarios (material known as 'marketing collateral' or 'sales-ready marketing').

The two functions should be able to work together in strategic planning cycles, where successful account planning relies on robust marketing plans and successful marketing plans rely on robust account plans. They should also be able to co-operate at an operational level. Take the example of a trade fair, where marketing wishes to generate an overall impression from the company stand and activities, and account managers need to meet buying decision-makers for specific discussions. It should never be assumed that marketing is only strategic and selling is only operational. Marketing and sales share responsibility for profitable revenue generation, so their interests should be closely aligned.

Back to TIX

In the context of the company's business strategy and marketing strategy, should TIX love and cherish its public-sector customer with high demands and low profits? TIX did decide to bid for the business, because to 'no bid' would have meant accepting a severe contraction in the size of the business, which would have meant a devastating adjustment to the 'MUST' objective promised to the shareholders. It would have affected the company's standing in the local business community and demotivated employees and investors. But they also knew that they had to use the new situation with this key account to facilitate growth and profitability. TIX was successful. What happened?

There were several reasons. They brought the best manufacturer of the new communication technology into their bid as a partner. They put a lot of resource into the bid to make sure every customer need was addressed in detail. They emphasized the TIX contribution to the local town. They committed extensive resources to the implementation of the new technology so that problems could be resolved quickly.

There was a long-term payoff. The previously grumpy customer was impressed and acted as a highly entertaining reference account. This is the classic case of growth through a key account. Because TIX did embrace the ambition of the customer for a new technology, the company became an attractive supplier to other organizations who wanted to take on the risks of the new platform in return for its cost-saving potential. TIX won new customers with reduced sales and marketing costs.

There were concerns about the erosion of the value of the deal to both parties over such a long period as 10 years, which is a very long time in information technology, so reviews and rebids were scheduled. The managed service agreement proved to be more profitable than the previous maintenance and service contract, because TIX had much more control of upgrades.

Through a thoughtful, strategic approach, the key account, which had been in jeopardy, contributed to the achievement of business growth objectives, and account profitability was also improved.

Closing thoughts

The detail of a bid to a key account may seem a long way removed from the corporate growth strategy, but it is not. Strategy is the allocation of scarce resources to opportunities. If a bid is critical to a company growth objective, the sales manager needs to pull in the best resources, and adopt the best tactics, to make it a winning bid. There is no bottom line for shareholders unless there is a prosperous top line driven by marketing and sales. The top line does not happen unless there are customers convinced that the company is the best at meeting their needs. In the case of key accounts, that takes a huge amount of effort. This means that most companies can only manage a limited number of key accounts. In the next chapter, we examine how key accounts can be distinguished from non-key accounts.

Action list

Things to note or find out:

How is my company's sales target split between the Ansoff quadrants?

What is our approach to doing more with our smaller customers online?

Are we clear about how many key accounts we can manage?

How does my key account plan fit in with other plans in the business?

How well do I work with marketing, and marketing with me?

References

Ansoff, HI (1957) Strategies for diversification, *Harvard Business Review*, **35** (5), pp 113–24

Loren, G (2005) Dow Corning big pricing gamble, *Strategy+Innovation*, 7 March

McDonald, M and Rogers, B (1998) *Key Account Management: Learning from supplier and customer perspectives*, Butterworth-Heinemann, Oxford

McDonald, M and Wilson, H (2011) *Marketing Plans: How to prepare them, how to use them*, John Wiley & Sons, Chichester

Piercy, N and Lane, N (2006) The underlying vulnerabilities in key account management strategies, *European Management Journal*, **24** (2), pp 151–62

Selecting the right key accounts

03

Key account management (KAM), to me, represents a collaborative approach to the buyer/seller exchange. It is the currency through which customers and suppliers extract value that goes far deeper than transactional relationships.

From the seller's side, it helps to neutralize competition, shorten timelines and sure-up forecasts. KAM starts during the initial sales pursuit, when the customer commits to embark on a journey with a strategic supplier. Active customer participation is an integral part of how my team sells 'value' and it helps set us apart from the competition.

If you want your initiative to succeed then:

- **Don't presume that your current biggest customers are those most worthy of KAM attention** (instead promote those accounts with the biggest *potential* to add value).

- **Or that every customer wants to be key account** (you have to ask customers if they want to participate in the programme).

- **Remember that KAM is not for transactional relationships and neither is it an excuse to offer lower pricing to 'key' accounts** (some of your largest customers will demand the lowest prices yet continue to treat you as a commodity supplier).

- **Rethink your compensation structure to reward appropriate behaviour** (KAM success does not happen overnight so consider how you will target individuals in the short to medium term).

- **Incorporate KAM within a wider sales and marketing framework such as ABM** (KAM is a way to extract value from marketing, not a marketing strategy in its own right).

David Lucas-Smith, Enterprise Sales Director for a
NASDAQ 100 technology company

This is a worthy quote from a sales director to start our consideration of the foundations of successful KAM. As with Chapter 2, we begin this chapter with a real-world case study. At the end of the chapter we then provide guidance on the way forward.

CASE STUDY   Finsberg Financial Services

Jill Smith works for Finsberg Financial Services as the key account manager for a multinational food company. Finsberg specializes in providing insurance for customers with high risks, such as storing explosive materials, or product integrity risks in their supply chains. Key account teams include highly sought-after underwriters.

Jill gets a call from the chief executive of a large city council. She is a second connection on LinkedIn. He has recently taken over and wants to streamline the supplier base. He was looking for new suppliers and asked a few contacts for ideas. Although it is not normal in the cash-strapped public sector, he wants a more partnership approach with approved suppliers, including long contracts and the opportunity to add value in innovative ways. A large number of contracts will be advertised for competitive tender, and he would like Finsberg to submit a bid for a portfolio of financial services. To work with such a major city council would be high profile, and potentially generate a lot of revenue for a long period of time. It is unusual to get such a high-profile decision-maker proactively seeking a bid, so clearly there is some potential for success.

Finsberg does have growth targets and would not usually turn down the opportunity to work with a customer who likes the brand. However, the company has always focused on its specialism. Although public-sector organizations do need to insure for considerable risks, Finsberg does not currently have any other city councils as customers. The strategic fit is not obvious. Should Finsberg spend a lot of time and money bidding to the city council? Is this a potential key account, or a potential misfitting customer that would be a high cost to serve?

In Chapter 2, we positioned KAM alongside professional marketing strategy and explored a variety of routes to profitable growth. KAM is clearly a major input to revenue and profit and has to be managed as professionally as any other major capability in the organization.

Furthermore, there are some extremely large customers that suppliers have to deal with, either because of the revenue they are able to provide, or because of their reputation in the market. In most markets, however, there is a substantial choice of large customers, and if any of them are to be included in a special, separately administered KAM programme then one of the main issues to face is how many and which to include.

In Chapter 1 we made a case for limiting the number of key accounts, but how can those happy few be selected?

Different types of relationships

Even large organizations can become over-reliant on their key accounts. If a key account is worth more than 10 per cent of your turnover, it is a sign that strategy needs to shift to developing new key accounts from other parts of the customer portfolio (as discussed in Chapter 1). In order to balance risk, it is important to have a balanced customer portfolio and focus resources only where integrated relationships are robustly justified. Sometimes, you have to know when to stop developing an account. A global distribution company known to the authors had 18 such relationships and each one was more profitable than any single country. The problem was that this supplier then tried to develop 100. They just could not resource that many, and eventually reverted to a much lower number.

When selecting which customers and potential customers should be included in your key account programme, there will inevitably be a mix of different kinds of relationships. Thinking about Finsberg (the opening case study), where their prospect is talking about partnership prior to any existing relationship, could this be a ploy by the customer to encourage a proposal offering investments in their organization, which reduce their risk but increase Finsberg's risks?

Although it can be a challenging procedure, it is important to categorize all customer relationships in a logical and businesslike way in order to manage each one appropriately for the purpose of generating the desired level of profitability, which will result in shareholder value added.

The next section of this chapter will explain in detail how to do this. *This is the most crucial chapter in the book, for the result of this process will determine everything that follows, including the setting of objectives and strategies for each key account, as well as plans and resourcing.*

> In order to balance risk, it is important to have a balanced customer portfolio and focus resources only where integrated relationships are robustly justified.

Classifying your key accounts

The matrix in Figure 3.1 has a fancy name, but do not be put off. We promise you that it is very practical, actionable and useful. From here on, we will refer to it as the SPM (strategic planning matrix).

Figure 3.1   Selecting and categorizing customers by potential

```
                        Supplier business strength with customer
                            High                    Low
              High  ┌──────────────────┬──────────────────┐
                    │    Strategic     │    Selective     │
                    │   investment     │   investment     │
                    │                  │                  │
                    │    Strategic     │      Star        │
   Account          ├──────────────────┼──────────────────┤
 attractiveness     │    Proactive     │    Management    │
                    │   maintenance    │    for cash      │
                    │                  │                  │
                    │     Status       │    Streamline    │
              Low   └──────────────────┴──────────────────┘
```

SOURCE adapted from Woodburn and McDonald (2012)

The purpose of the McDonald/Rogers KAM strategic planning matrix (SPM) is to map all important key customers relative to each other in the context of:

- the relative attractiveness of each for your future;
- the relative competitiveness of your company in each key customer;

- the relative contribution of each to your future turnover and profits;

- provide a basis for setting realistic objectives and strategies to achieve your objectives.

A by-product of this planning exercise is the ability to explain your firm's strategy clearly and unequivocally to your stakeholders.

Please note: change the criteria, scores and weights to suit your company's circumstances and objectives. People often ask us for 'the right formula'. It would be quite wrong to say that one formula works for all companies. We do urge all companies to include customer profitability as an attractiveness factor, but it would rarely be the only factor that mattered. In Chapter 1, we looked at overall business objectives and strategies, and these should influence selection criteria. For example, volume is highly weighted by process manufacturers, because it helps to keep the factory running 24/7. A professional services company that works from project to project probably weights profitability highly. Account attractiveness factors can also vary according to company size. Larger companies value volume, because they have a certain scope to sustain. Smaller companies are usually looking for key accounts that will help them to grow. In the case of Finsberg, in addition to volume and profitability we might expect to see 'strategic fit' as an attractiveness factor, based on the account having high risks to manage.

The process for completing the SPM is as follows:

Step 1

The first step is to select the accounts to be included in this process. If you have a powerful CRM analytics system, you can probably apply selection criteria to your entire customer base. However, for the purpose of conceptualizing account selection for the first time, we suggest initially confining the list to 10 or less actual or potential key accounts. Be open-minded about the accounts to be included. It doesn't matter at this stage if the account is a target rather than a current customer. This step is of crucial importance and you must think about the prospect of growing your profits over the next three years, not just next year.

Consider the example in Table 3.1. We refer to the amount of money the customer (or target) spends on the type of products/services you offer as 'wallet size' in this table. For example, if you are a paper company selling to a pharmacy chain, and they spend £4 million every year on paper products, then £4 million is their wallet size.

Table 3.1 Comparing size of wallet in key accounts (example)

Key account/target name	'Wallet size' for our range in £ million per year	Our current share of wallet (%)
ABC	4	90
DEF	10	10
GHI	20	15
JKL	6	80
MNO	14	75
PQR	30	12
STU	10	60
VWX	10	63
YZA	24	45
BCD	8	80

So you have now selected your 10 key accounts.

Step 2

When selecting key accounts, particularly if they are channel intermediaries, selection criteria should include the sustainability of that relationship and the potential lifetime value of that account. Customers are subjected to rigorous selection criteria, through a form of due diligence, in order to be selected as a key account. The ultimate success of the relationship depends upon resources being invested in that account, and investing resources in the right accounts is critical to our long-term success.

Darren Bayley, Commercial Director, Dentsply Sirona

Now you have to list your 10 key accounts on a kind of thermometer, with 'high' at the top and 'low' at the bottom. 'High' will mean those accounts that offer the best prospect for any relevant competitor (not just you) to grow their profit over the next three years, so we will label this vertical axis: 'Account Attractiveness'. In order to do this dispassionately, you will need a logical set of criteria, as suggested by Darren Bayley in the quote above. An example is shown in Table 3.2.

Table 3.2 A scoring system for account attractiveness (example)

Account Attractiveness Factors		Scoring System (out of 10)		
Factor	Weight	1–3	4–6	7–10
Current volume shipped	40	2–3 lorry-loads per week	2–3 full lorry-loads per day	Multiple full lorry-loads per day
Their growth rate in their sector	10	Under 10% in last 3 years	10–20% in last 3 years	10–20% in last year
Profitability of business/potential business with this customer (after overheads, interest and depreciation are applied)	20	1–3%	4–6%	7–10%
Organizational 'fit'	30	Limited process integration	Shared data and automation of processes	Fully integrated supply chains systems
	100			

SOURCE adapted from McDonald and Rogers (1998)

Several decision-makers in the company must sit and think through what makes a customer strategically important to the business. In the example in Table 3.2, four attractiveness factors have been chosen, which are typical of many companies' interests when comparing key accounts. Note that only one tries to capture future potential, ie the customer's growth rate in their sector. Making analyses forward looking is very difficult, but some attempt should be made to look forwards rather than backwards.

Referring again to Table 3.2 you now have to decide which of the three or four account attractiveness factors you have chosen is less or more important (we refer to this as 'weighting'). For example, if you have a factory and have only 40 per cent occupancy, you might decide to give volume a higher weight than profitability. On the other hand, if you are working at full capacity, you may decide to give profitability a higher weight than volume.

Different decision-makers may have different priorities. An operations director may be more interested in volume than the finance director, who is keen on profitability per customer. All stakeholders need to be involved in deciding the weightings, but the weightings used must represent what is strategic to the company overall.

Step 3

On the right-hand side of Table 3.2, you can see an example scoring system. The next step is to decide how you are going to score key accounts against your weighted criteria. Once again, several stakeholders need to agree how relative attractiveness can be determined.

Step 4

Table 3.3   Scoring key account attractiveness (example)

Account Attractiveness Factors		Key Accounts					
Factor	Weight	ABC		DEF		GHI	
Current volume shipped	40	9	360	3	120	4	160
Their growth rate in their sector	10	4	40	8	80	7	70
Profitability of business/potential business	20	5	100	8	160	6	120
Organizational 'fit'	30	9	270	6	90	5	150
	100		770		450		500

SOURCE adapted from Rogers (2007)

Score each key customer according to the parameters you have used in Table 3.3. Then multiply their score by the weight (also in Table 3.3). You can see how high scores on low-weighted factors can be counteracted by low scores on factors that are more important.

Draw a box of your own based on Figure 3.1. Place each key customer on the vertical line of the box, with scores from low to high. Ensure that you use scale to reflect the spread of scores, rather than absolute numbers. For example, if the lowest score is 350, make the vertical axis start at 300. If the highest score is 750, make 800 the highest point on the scale. This will ensure that each of your 10 accounts is spread out on the scale.

It is also important to remember that an account lower down the vertical axis is not necessarily 'unattractive'. It merely means that it is less attractive than one higher up the vertical axis in its ability to grow your profits over the next three years.

Step 5

Evaluate your strengths in each key account relative to your most relevant competitor. Do this intuitively first of all, supported by the message you perceive in your 'share of wallet'. If share of wallet is more than 50 per cent, then competitive strength must be high, and if it is less it must be at the low end of the scale. Take care to note that 'low' is on the *right-hand side* of the matrix. Then see if you can get the customer to give you detailed information, as illustrated in Step 6.

Customers have their own view of whether you are strategic to their business and, in particular, new entrants simply don't figure in their plans. If you can get an audience with the key decision-makers, it is highly likely they will give you a series of credibility tests involving low-value, non-critical opportunities, with little or no risk to their business. Purchasing people like to make safe buying decisions, so they are not going to award a major contract overnight. Frequently it takes years to build up credibility.

Paul Beaumont, Interim Sales Director

It is also important to remember that an account lower down the vertical axis is not necessarily 'unattractive'. It merely means that it is less attractive than one higher up the vertical axis in its ability to grow your profits over the next three years.

Step 6

Table 3.4 How a key account rates suppliers (example)

Customer YZA's Critical Success Factors		Our Score Versus Competitors'					
Factor	Weight	Us		Comp A		Comp B	
Price	20	6	120	9	180	4	80
Delivery	40	9	360	3	120	6	240
Quality	20	7	140	7	140	8	160
Innovation	10	3	30	5	50	9	90
Range	10	7	70	8	80	3	30
	100		720		570		600

SOURCE adapted from McDonald and Rogers (1998)

A good measure of the seriousness that the customer pays to the supplier relationship is whether a dedicated supplier procurement manager is assigned to us.

Steve Jackson, Business Development Manager for a global manufacturing and services company

For the scoring on the horizontal axis in Figure 3.1 to be objective, you have to see your qualities as a supplier from each customer's point of view. Ideally, you need the information shown in Table 3.4 – how you score against competitors per weighted buying criterion. What is most important to them for this category of purchase? How do they score you against your nearest competitors? We can see in Table 3.4 that customer YZA weighted delivery highly, and if we are beating competitors on that then our competitive strength is going to be high. We could improve on other factors if we want to achieve more share of wallet. Remember that each key account will have different criteria, so this exercise hase to be done for each key account – normally by the key account manager.

Step 7

Now find the points of intersection for each of your 10 key accounts on the four-box matrix that you have drawn using Figure 3.1.

Step 8

You will now have a variety of dots in your box, each representing a key account. You can increase the size of the dot to reflect the relative size of the key account's current spend on your product/service range.

Step 9

Set objectives and strategies for these key accounts using our guidelines for each of the four boxes (see Table 3.5).

Table 3.5 Typical objectives and strategies for the quadrants of the McDonald/ Rogers KAM strategic planning matrix (SPM)

Account Type	Potential Objectives	Potential Strategies	Other Considerations
Strategic	Secure future development projects and invest; sustain or incrementally grow volume/ revenue	When business is already this good, the only way to grow is by helping the customer to grow. Through shared strategic planning, opportunities to introduce new products or enter new markets can be considered.	Consider the risks inherent in this business. Does it represent a high proportion of your revenue? Should you invest more in other customers to diversify your portfolio?
Status	Sustain volume, revenue and profitability	These accounts should be defended from competitors, but not at any cost. Relationship development is still important.	Where there is a mismatch in supplier and customer intentions, it is not always a problem.

(continued)

Table 3.5 (*Continued*)

Account Type	Potential Objectives	Potential Strategies	Other Considerations
Star	Gain account share, but be selective about investments in bids	Knowing when to invest in a star is difficult. They are happy with another supplier. Taking small bits of business that the incumbent does not want can help to build account share.	Keeping in contact with the customer while waiting for the incumbent supplier to make a major mistake is also a viable strategy.
Streamline	Minimize costs to serve; maximize cash flow	Usually the customers will be happy enough with standard products and ease-of-doing-business – by telephone account management or ordering via a portal.	Staff in call centres must be well-trained enough to spot when the customer's purchasing activity is scaling up.

SOURCE adapted from Woodburn and McDonald (2012)

As discussed earlier, every company will develop its own system of key account selection based on its own objectives and outlook. Here are some thoughts from an experienced senior manager, and we think you will see how they align with the process discussed in this chapter:

The starting point for many organizations in selecting key accounts is the value of business, in terms of revenue and sales that has been secured (past tense). Whilst this is understandable, and inevitable to some extent, it is seldom sufficient for an enduring long-term profitable relationship to develop and be maintained. Other criteria should include:

- The macroeconomic context of the potential key account: does this look favourable in the medium to long term (in terms of stability and growth)?

- Does the potential key account have a strong, long-term and (ideally) growing need for the services and products the supplier offers?

- Is there scope for cross- and up-selling a wide range of services and products?

- Is the potential key account stable, mature, with strong governance and of good reputational standing?

- Are the corporate cultures of the potential key account and supplier compatible, with a joint sense of values and purpose?

- Are the personal relationships between key individuals in both organizations strong, or capable of becoming strong and enduring?

- For large multinational companies, potential key accounts will probably need to have a global footprint in providing sufficient scope and scale for a long-term profitable relationship.

- The potential key account's view of the supplier is also important. There needs to be a degree of mutuality in organizations regarding their relationship and each other as strategic, because without this a strong relationship is unlikely to develop.

- Ultimately, there will be a financial measure or threshold in justifying the investment needed in setting up the KAM systems and infrastructure. For global key accounts, this threshold can be in the tens of millions of pounds as a starting point in creating a sufficient basis for business case.

Mature supplier organizations will usually segment their customer base so that the appropriate investments and focus can be applied in maximizing the returns. In the context of account management, a potential key account may start life as a *'target account'* because they meet most, or all, of the criteria described above, with the exception of meeting the financial threshold. A *'target account'* will become a key account when it passes the financial threshold. Typically a key account will retain its status until it stops providing growth. It may well still be a substantial account and remain so for a long time to come, but growth is important, and a lack of it will usually mean that the key account is relegated and becomes an 'anchor account'. Inevitably a lack of growth becomes a decline in revenue and if this continues the anchor account will be relegated again, this time to a *'transactional account'*. With a decline in status, as the account moves through the life cycle, there is a corresponding decline in investment, service levels and responsiveness and, ultimately, a decision is made as to whether it makes sense to serve the customer at all.

Simon Derbyshire, Vice-President of Capgemini Saudi Arabia
*Capgemini: a global leader in consulting, technology
and outsourcing services*

Note that Simon discusses selection criteria and the progression of accounts from target to key, and how accounts can decline in status as well, as discussed in relation to Figure 3.2.

Risk of exit

All companies should be prepared to manage the transition of key accounts to non-key and to manage the risk of key accounts switching to a competitor. It does happen. The primary causes are changes in strategic direction of either the supplier or the customer, or 'negative critical incidents' (NCIs) – we are sure that you can find a colloquial term for what we mean! An NCI is when something goes wrong... such as:

- Poor handling of a change of key personnel (in either company, or a partner).
- Breach of trust – something was promised but did not happen. The breach can come from either party.
- Misuse of power – such as the customer demanding an excessive discount.
- Complacency.
- Cultural mismatch between organizations (eg bureaucracies with entrepreneurial customers or vice versa).
- Quality problems with the product or service.
- Financial problems (especially the customer's failure to pay on time).
- Either the supplier or customer loses their status in their sector.

Close business relationships can have a dark side. This is why selecting a customer for special resource allocation must be done very carefully, and why the quality of the relationship should be monitored closely and re-examined periodically.

All companies should be prepared to manage the transition of key accounts to non-key and to manage the risk of key accounts switching to a competitor.

The importance of correct selection

The examples below illustrate the more difficult cases you will come across. Ultimately, deep knowledge of each account is needed in addition to data. Objectivity is important, but data is not insight. Insight is generated when data provokes analytical and creative thinking.

Example 1

Customer Ainsworth & Bibury SA was a massive, global publishing company that had decided to rationalize its paper suppliers, choosing only two who would give them the lowest price.

One of their suppliers (Supplier Snow Inc) was a big player in the market and they had high fixed costs in their paper mills. They could not afford to lose the substantial volume of paper production that Ainsworth & Bibury represented, as their fixed costs would remain and have to be spread over a much reduced volume, making all their products uncompetitive.

So, Snow Inc entered the bidding process in order to win the contract, even at a ridiculously low price. When they had won their unattractive contract, they stuck to the terms of the contract and charged extra for anything outside the contract, as well as minimizing the costs to serve this customer. Ainsworth & Bibury had slumped from strategic account to the borderline between status and streamline.

The point of the story is that it may well be that there is a big, important customer that does not offer much potential for growth in profits but has to be kept. Reducing costs to serve is the only way forward in this case, followed by vigorous attempts to diversify the customer portfolio. Of course, if Snow Inc was a services company, where most costs are variable, they might be very happy to lose Ainsworth & Bibury to a competitor.

Example 2

Company Wyvert Ltd had a big, attractive client (Customer Feedwelk GmbH) with an annual spend of £32 million in their product category, which was growing year by year. The problem for Wyvert was that they were rated by Feedwelk as the worst of all suppliers and had a tiny share of that £32 million spend. The reason for this was that the Wyvert 'system' was showing Feedwelk as a small customer, which was encouraging profit maximization. A review of the wider potential in Feedwelk would have informed Wyvert that they should have been investing in Feedwelk in order to increase account share.

It was only by positioning Feedwelk in the context of all the other clients in a SPM that the senior managers became aware of the counter-productive nature of that 'streamline' account strategy, and switched to a 'star' approach.

Time factors in business relationships

In the early days of KAM, researchers were keen to observe how relationships developed over time. It is very important to remember that key accounts were not always key accounts and are not always going to be key accounts. One of the most convincing research articles we have seen argued on the basis of a large sample that most business relationships are at their best in the growth phase. Research from the purchasers' point of view demonstrates concern about over-commitment to key suppliers, so decline is always possible once the planned benefits of close partnership have matured (see Figure 3.2).

- Exploratory KAM is where a customer has been identified as a potential key account, but trading between the two companies is limited. Both sides are exploring each other's capability. The supplier is building their reputation as a potential challenger to the competitor who currently has the majority share of the customer's spend in this category of goods/services.

- Basic KAM is mainly transactional and the supplier needs to prove their efficiency and reliability. Price is frequently important to the customer at this stage and the supplier is likely to be only one of many others. It is easy for the customer to exit the relationship, but there is also the opportunity to grow the business by

Figure 3.2 Life cycle of supplier–customer relationships

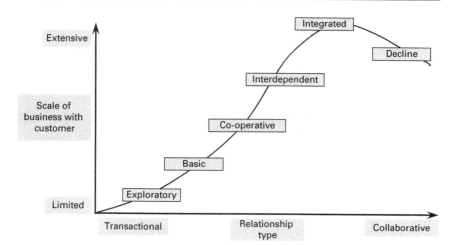

SOURCE adapted from Millman and Wilson (1995); Jap and Anderson (2007)

demonstrating reliability on the core criteria of price, quality and delivery. A challenger can gain a reputation for being 'easy to do business with'.

- Co-operative KAM is a stage whereby the supplier is one of a few 'preferred' by the customer. There are multiple contact points between supplier personnel and customer personnel, although the main relationship is still with the professional purchasing team. There is limited information sharing and the supplier is not fully trusted by the customer. It is often at this stage that the supplier trades unprofitably in pursuit of 'account share'. Ideally, key account managers aspire to move the relationship forward to interdependence. If that is not going to happen due to the way the customer buys (see Chapter 4) it is probably better to move the relationship back to a basic one and focus on the core delivery promise. The costs of managing a co-operative relationship should be closely monitored.

- Interdependent KAM reflects a much closer relationship between supplier and customer and both acknowledge the strategic impor-tance to each other. The supplier may even be the sole supplier for a particular category of goods or services. There will certainly be lots of information sharing and a degree of cross-organizational trust (respect for each other's brand values) and cross-contact trust (respect between individual professionals) will emerge. There will be joint strategic planning and excellent opportunities to grow the business. Such relationships are difficult to develop and will be few in number.

- Integrated KAM involves both supplier and customer working almost as one single organization in the process of creating value for both parties. Such is the level of interrelationships between the business that exit becomes quite difficult, even traumatic. Cross-functional project teams on both sides work on specific projects, often using transparent costing systems. Such relationships can be very profitable for both parties, but are very difficult to develop. However, it is not uncommon to see co-branded logistics, or IT solutions (eg 'Intel Inside'), and it is often for the benefit of the end customer that players in supply chains integrate their product development and operations. Integrated relationships can be controversial, as they can be seen as quasi joint ventures, which would normally be subject to intense due diligence and shareholder review. And, of course, should such a relationship have to be disintegrated at any time, the risks and costs are considerable.

- Key account relationships may decline gradually as mutual commercial interests between supplier and customer diverge, or they may be hit by crises – either external ones such as recessions or internal, such as a public relations scandal affecting one party. It is always prudent for both parties to agree an exit plan for both decline and crisis scenarios.

Key account managers aspire to move the relationship forward to interdependence. If that is not going to happen due to the way the customer buys, it is probably better to move the relationship back to a basic one and focus on the core delivery promise.

The concept of developing key account relationships over time and across these categories is a useful one in key account planning (discussed in Chapter 5). Its importance here is to show that once a selection exercise has been done, it tells you something about how you need to develop relationships with particular key accounts or target key accounts. They do not have to stand still at the point in time that you do the analysis. The main reason for doing the analysis is to raise awareness of accounts that are not so key as had been thought, and to identify accounts that are missed opportunities, and then change things for the better.

Having spent many years in sales and account management, devising strategies to build strong bonds with my customers, I am now a technology innovation investor and I get to see the picture from the other side. I have come across many examples of bad KAM; in fact within my sector there are examples of misunderstandings of sales itself. Helping start-ups understand about sales and relationship management is challenging and one aspect that continues to be misunderstood is that innovation does not sell itself. It requires a proactive, positive approach not only to understanding the market but also to understanding the value that the innovation delivers for a customer. Too often a great technological achievement can be sat on a shelf due to lack of sales effort.

It is not just start-ups that have difficulty understanding how to build business relationships. A number of large companies seem to have adopted the mantra of 'delight the customer' – in other words, 'do whatever the customer says, regardless' and call it KAM. This puts the balance of power with the customer. Suppliers end up focusing too heavily on a few key accounts, keeping them delighted, while the key accounts keep their options open. If a problem occurs and the relationship breaks down, then the supplier is in serious trouble. A collaboration is built when supplier and customer jointly develop a new product, but the real strategic impact is when they work together to take it to market. Then both companies can focus less on managing each other and focus more on managing a shared future. Even then, there is still a need for the key account manager to work hard to sustain success.

Andy Proctor, Innovation Lead, InnovateUK

Avoiding pitfalls

Several research papers identify failings in the selection of key accounts as a primary cause of problems in KAM programmes.

We have found the following to be the most common defects in key account selection:

- Lists too long are unmanageable in practice, resulting in a failure to deliver the value promised (spreading the service too thinly).

- Lists being literally just that – 'lists' resulting in a lack of any kind of strategic guidance or difference. We have heard of the customer portfolio simply being divided among the sales professionals in ad hoc ways.

- The process of selection itself hinders the inclusion of potential new key accounts. In practice, this problem can be overcome by assessing the accounts to be included in the KAM programme at least once a year at the beginning of the annual planning cycle.

- Frequently there is internal, political pressure to include unsuitable accounts for a host of reasons. The most frequent is the longevity of the trading relationship, the status of a customer in their sector, or because a particular customer has always been a favourite of a senior manager.

> Can we disaggregate fact-based evidence (*in the real world*) from high aspirational goals? All too often I have seen CEOs and directors impose a list of key accounts on a sales team in the forlorn hope that the 'A team' will deliver the results (*after all, that's what they do isn't it?*).
>
> Contribution from a key account manager in the manufacturing sector

The biggest problem of all, however, in our view, is the inclusion of customers based solely on current results rather than on future potential.

The selection of key accounts has a big impact on the success of the entire KAM programme. Companies need to have the right criteria, the right data and the judgement to make the right decisions.

And finally...

Now let's return to Jill Smith and Finsberg. The local government prospect may be offering a large chunk of business, but it is likely that their activities are being cut by central government and they will be price sensitive, so the potential for profit is limited. Organizational fit will be limited, because Finsberg does not currently have public-sector customers. So this is a potential misfitting customer that would be a high cost to serve. It seems reasonable to suggest a 'no bid' in this situation, unless Finsberg is considering diversifying into a new sector and could use this as a pilot case.

We hope you have now managed to work out the different potential for your own top accounts. Correct selection is incredibly important. In our experience, when companies start a quest for objectivity in categorizing their customers, the first benefit is that they stop wasting money on customers who do not want partnership relationships with them. Avoiding that waste then creates time and resources to invest in truly strategic opportunities. The way in which these can be planned is explored later in the book. Chapter 4 explores the purchasing profession and its influence on the success or otherwise of key account objectives and strategies.

Action list

Set aside some time to work through the selection process outlined in this chapter and work through some examples.

If information is missing, see if there is a way of getting it.

References

Jap, SD and Anderson, E (2007) Testing a life-cycle theory of cooperative interorganizational relationships: movement across stages and performance, *Management Science*, 53 (2), pp 260–75

McDonald, M and Rogers, B (1998) *Key Account Management: Learning from supplier and customer perspectives*, Butterworth-Heinemann, Oxford

Millman, T and Wilson, K (1995) From key account selling to key account management, *Journal of Marketing Practice: Applied marketing science*, 1 (1), pp 9–21

Rogers, B (2007) *Rethinking Sales Management: A strategic guide for practitioners*, John Wiley & Sons, Chichester

Woodburn, D and McDonald, M (2012) *Key Account Management: The definitive guide*, John Wiley & Sons, Chichester

Understanding buying decisions

04

Clearly, as a senior leader in a global business with purchasing authority for nearly €10 million of spend across Europe on telecoms, I was an important person to the Head of Corporate Sales (EMEA) at (telecoms company). But, and it's a crucial but, just because I was important to him didn't mean he was important to me. I understand my importance as a customer from the fact that I have €10 million to spend. Why, though, does the fact that I spend €10 million in a marketplace make any particular salesperson more important to me than any other salesperson, or even important enough for me to want to spend time with them?

Rob Maguire, Procurement Consultant and Partner of MaguireIzatt (www.maguireizatt.co.uk). Extract from a published chapter (Maguire, 2017)

Again, we start this chapter with a real-life case study and, at the end of the chapter, we suggest a way forward.

CASE STUDY Qualität GmbH

Qualität GmbH (known globally as QG) was spun off from a major conglomerate 10 years ago, but one former sister company (Zuverlässigkeit AG, known as ZLK) is still its most important key account. Having been part of the same group, processes are integrated, and relationships between senior managers have always been cordial. Into this cosy business partnership steps Heine Schmitt, the new purchasing manager for ZLK. He has a professional approach to supplier management, and is determined to reduce the supplier base and make sure that those that pass his tests will price competitively or innovate with ZLK to deliver future product lines. Of course, the directors who took him on assumed that he would only axe small suppliers. But Heine knows that having too many 'strategic suppliers' is also costly, especially if they are complacent.

He soon gets to hear anecdotes about QG's complacency from several sources – inaccurate calculations on transactions, over-priced and under-delivered services, partial deliveries, a relatively junior employee as account manager and so on. He is cautious. The managing directors of the two companies still play golf together. Heine disapproves of hospitality between supplier and customer, but he knows that he needs to shake up QG without upsetting his new boss.

Heine decides to call QG's sales director to suggest a review meeting. The sales director's PA offers him the key account manager. Heine is infuriated. He asks his up-and-coming junior buyer to research all of QG's shortcomings evident from internal data, and to evaluate the offering of QG's two main competitors. Then he talks to the key account manager, laying out all the evidence in front of him. Because he is indeed junior, the key account manager cannot respond, but offers to go back to his superiors to try to develop a response. 'You do that', says Heine. 'You've got three days before I pick up the phone to your competitors.'

Customer power

Why are customers today so powerful? Arguably, the business world in the 1950s and 1960s was fairly complacent. Markets had been growing and it is easy to succeed in growth markets. The 1970s brought the shock of the oil crisis and the growth of information technology. By the mid-1980s, the globalization of business offered purchasing professionals a whole new world of potential sources of supply and opportunities to dramatically reduce their cost base. Purchasing has rapidly evolved from being an administrative to a strategic function over the past 40 years – for a simple reason. If your spending on purchases is 60 per cent and your profit is 5 per cent, and you cut your spending on purchases to 55 per cent, your profits double to 10 per cent. Costs saved on purchases go straight to the bottom line.

Consultants A.T. Kearney, in their 2014 Global Assessment of Excellence in Procurement study, found that companies who lead the way in procurement gain measureable cost reductions twice those of average companies (Blaskovic, Ferrer and Easton (2014)). Procurement excellence involves achieving business performance through managing categories, suppliers and buying teams. Obviously buyers have had to manage risks as well as costs as they have taken on the new strategic role of purchasing, and they have needed suppliers who could accompany them on the journey.

> *Costs saved on purchases go straight to the bottom line.*

In fact, purchasing decisions-makers have been demanding a change from the unsophisticated selling of previous decades. They want to discuss their finances, their business processes, their organization and their culture. They want suppliers who can offer them routes to competitive advantage, not just products.

In many industries, there has been a growing trend to see a small number of global leaders. It has been difficult for the 'second tier' to compete with them because of their economies of scale and scope. The result of all of this has been a dramatic shift in the balance of power from suppliers to customers, so it is important to understand how customers buy and what they consider to be important.

Defining the customer

> The ability of the key account manager to see and understand the world from the customer's point of view, as well as their own, is central to being able to build a truly sustainable and value-creating relationship.
>
> Darren Bayley, Commercial Director, Dentsply Sirona

It is important to understand who the customer is. Below is an example of a conversation about account definition:

'So which key account are we talking about?'

'Zapata.'

'All of it?'

'Yes.'

'Including paper towels, nappies, clothing protection, sanitary products and incontinence products?'

'No, just incontinence products.'

'So, it is all of Zapata's incontinence products division, worldwide?'

'No, we only deal with Europe.' Pause. 'Well, a few countries in Western Europe.'

'So, what proportion of Zapata's spend on our product category is that?'

'Sorry, I haven't a clue.'

The smaller and smaller the parts of the global company that you serve, the more vulnerable you are to delisting.

Figure 4.1 illustrates a frequent misunderstanding on the part of suppliers about their power. It shows the mistaken belief that they have 100 per cent of the available wallet, whereas the customer looked at the supplier in a different light and knew that this particular supplier had only 17 per cent of the available wallet or, at best, 29 per cent. Suppliers should have their marketing departments digging for information about customers that reveals the full category potential.

Figure 4.1   Defining the customer's 'wallet'

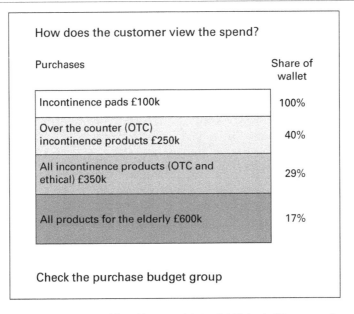

SOURCE adapted from M McDonald teaching material, Cranfield School of Management

Some suppliers and customers dealing with each other are very complex. There has been a tendency in the past 20 years for groups to centralize purchasing. Some suppliers have responded with centralized global account divisions. Clearly, the customer has increased their power if they centralize their buying, whilst the supplier continues to sell in a decentralized way. For smaller companies selling into larger companies, the centralization of purchasing can be an advantage, because to win any business could mean growing with the customer across its many divisions and geographies. However, only if you can cope with the implications for potential loss of control to remote agents and stretching the cash flow.

The notion of 'the buyer' is also misleading. We will discuss purchasing professionals, as they are extremely important and frequently are the ones who make the final decision. Nonetheless, purchasing professionals, or 'buyers' as we will call them, have been trained to take account of the views of those in their organization who will either use the purchased products or services or who will be impacted by them. On no account should key account managers try to 'go round' purchasing.

As a former purchasing manager, I can confirm that purchasing managers despise being deliberately sidelined and bypassed by key account managers. It is also a source of tension within a company as many managers want the ability to engage with whomever they want to work with, without the constraints of, or interference by, the purchasing department. This obviously undermines the purchasing function and company purchasing policy and processes. The reaction of the purchasing profession to key account managers' attempts to widen their network of contacts has included the adoption of digital and IT systems that put the supplier at arm's length, depriving them of face-to-face contact and once again exposing them to the prospect of commoditization and price-based arbitrage. In turn, key account managers are retaliating by using social and digital media – and so the cycle will continue.

There is, however, a more enlightened view that recognizes the symbiotic nature of the relationship that exists between customers and suppliers. In such relationships the role of, and relationship between, the purchasing manager and the key account manager is vital, not just to the functioning of the relationship, but also to the functioning of their respective

> businesses. In this setting the purchasing managers see the bigger picture. They understand that the real value that they can add to their own organization comes from deep integration with their strategic suppliers and creating an optimal match between demand and supply.
>
> Simon Derbyshire, Vice-President of Capgemini Saudi Arabia
>
> *Capgemini: a global leader in consulting,*
> *technology and outsourcing services*

An abiding method for understanding who these other influencers are is shown in Figure 4.2. This shows down the left-hand side a well-respected 10-step process that many organizations go through when they are buying expensive goods and services. The steps are simpler if it is a modified rebuy or a straight rebuy.

What is really interesting, however, about Figure 4.2 is the list of people or departments that might be affected by a particular purchase. This collection of people is often called the decision-making unit (DMU), but they do not behave like a single unit. They are a collection of stakeholders with different needs and expectations. For example, users of the product or service will clearly be keen to ensure that what is bought is the most appropriate to their needs, whilst accountants might be interested in any possible cost savings or cost avoidance. Notice the inclusion of a third-party expert to help with the purchase. Some companies outsource all of their purchasing function.

The kind of buying criteria that the DMU might consider are listed along the bottom of Figure 4.2. Of course, it can be difficult to access this information. Sometimes, purchasing managers will share it. Sometimes, some rigorous searching of company websites and LinkedIn for company organization charts and post-holders is needed. If your key accounts are small customers, do not assume that the entrepreneur who runs the business is the only decision-maker. He or she might have a trusted adviser at the local bank, or consult a member of the family as well as any key employees.

> *The decision-making unit (DMU) does not behave like a single unit. It comprises a collection of stakeholders with different needs and expectations.*

The authors ran a sales workshop for a components manufacturer in Australia, in which the topic of DMUs was covered in some depth. The company had bid for – but failed to win – a multimillion-dollar deal with a Japanese car manufacturer. We asked them to complete the data in Figure 4.2. They admitted that they had managed to get only 30 per cent of the right information to the right people. They consequently agreed that in future they would do this analysis for all major sales.

Figure 4.2   Analysing DMU involvement in the purchasing process (example)

Purchase Analysis						
Contact details for this contract: Sally Stone	Products/services being bought: Machine tools = Project Jupiter					
Decision-making unit:	Finance	Purchasing	End-user group	Operations	Health and Safety	External adviser
Buying-process stage:						
Needs identification			Joe Smith	Jenny Fletcher		
Need qualification		Sally Stone	Joe Smith			Jose Garcia
Detailed specification		Jan Weitz	Mahmood Ali	Jenny Fletcher	Dr Ben Graham	Jose Garcia
Supplier search		Jess Li				
Supplier qualification		Jan Weitz				Jose Garcia
Prepare tender documents	Theo Papas	Jan Weitz				
Evaluate proposals	Theo Papas	Zak Klein	Mahmood Ali	Jenny Fletcher	Dr Ben Graham	Jose Garcia
Negotiate terms	Theo Papas	Zak Klein Jan Weitz				
Finalize contract with chosen supplier		Jan Weitz				Lawyers: Brill & Gold
Monitor implementation			Joe Smith	Jenny Fletcher	Dr Ben Graham	
Decision considerations: Cost of ownership, payment terms, risk management, reliability of machines, service, guarantees, skills, partners, company reputation, joint investment funds, customer references						
Notes:						

SOURCE adapted from Malcolm McDonald Consulting material

Having identified the relevant influencers and their needs, it is important for potential suppliers to ensure that they get the right information to the right people at the right time. Purchasing will often want to make it difficult for suppliers to go direct to people in the DMU, but in the days of social media, companies need to be relaxed about informal contact development. If done appropriately, salespeople can ask for introductions to people who can explain their needs and then they can provide a better proposal. Of course, denying relationship building can backfire, particularly when it is counter-cultural.

> Some Western key accounts seem to purposefully accentuate the uncertainties felt by the Chinese supplier by having policies prohibiting the supplier from contacting more senior executives of the key account. This may be a strategic move, ie a means of keeping suppliers in constant fear of being made redundant and thus driven to accommodate demands...
>   ...advantages realized by blocking guanxi* may be short-lived...
> Chinese suppliers can be expected to have the option of turning much of their productive capacity to rising Chinese brands or to a growing array of Eastern key accounts from South Korea, Singapore, etc.
>
> Murphy and Li (2015: 1240)
>
> * A Chinese approach to relationship building.

The information imperative

It is argued these days that buyers are two-thirds of the way through a sale before they involve potential suppliers, and it is too late to start asking about problems and needs. Like many urban myths, this cannot be taken at face value. What we do know is that most consumers now search online before making a purchase and professional buyers do it as a matter of course. Before they engage with a potential supplier, they (or a junior colleague) will have trawled that company's website, industrial association websites, e-marketplaces, social media and search engines for all types of information about their performance in order to reduce risks inherent in the 'unknowns' of buying. They want to know the value-in-use of a supplier's solution, and what it feels like to be one of their customers. This is why incumbent suppliers often have an advantage. This type of information is usually only available after purchase and use of a product or service.

Account managers will need their marketing colleagues to get information about the company's strengths into every corner of the internet, including e-marketplaces, online trade shows, business-related social media and industry discussion groups, as well as the company website. For example, what manufacturing supplier can afford to ignore Applegate, the top destination for engineering buyers, which hosts over 400,000 suppliers and has recently partnered with the Chartered Institute of Purchasing and Supply (Donati, 2015)? Customer references and thought-leadership white papers or blogs are also essential online content. Without this kind of presence, account managers would have a hard time developing early credibility with buyers. Information also has to be easy to access and to evaluate. Purchasers in a hurry are not going to linger on sites that are slow or difficult to navigate.

> *They want to know the value-in-use of a supplier's solution, and what it feels like to be one of their customers.*

We know that purchasing decision-makers ask colleagues, fellow purchasers and other network contacts about a potential supplier's capabilities. The reason for the rise of the 'Net Promoter Score' (NPS) as a measurement of a company's success is rooted in the credibility of personal recommendations. Frederick Reichheld, who devised the NPS, said that it was the one figure you need to know before investing in a company (Reichheld and Markey, 2011). It tells you how many of their customers would recommend them to a contact, less the number who would not. Many companies in business and consumer sectors regularly conduct research on whether or not customers would recommend them. Who would want a negative NPS? Perceptions are critical. Meeting 'service level agreement' criteria means nothing if the customer perceives that you only did the bare minimum to avoid contractual penalties. On paper you did your bit. In the mind of the customer, you broke the spirit of the agreement.

> *Meeting 'service level agreement' criteria means nothing if the customer perceives that you only did the bare minimum to avoid contractual penalties.*

Price and value

Professional buyers are not just part of the buying DMU, they are usually driving it. Since the 1980s, purchasing professionals have been taught to examine the total cost of ownership (see Table 4.1) and the whole value chain in which they operate. They are interested in buying goods and services that will help their organizations reduce costs, avoid costs, or add value to their offers to their own customers. However, nothing is as simple as it seems.

In Table 4.1 we can see that a widget costing twice the price of another may incur much lower value-in-use costs over its lifetime. On this evidence, we would expect the higher-price widget to be preferred.

Table 4.1   Examining the total cost of ownership

Total cost of ownership per widget in $	Company 1	Company 2
80	Breakages	
70	Downtime	
60	Cost of disposal	
50	Cost of	Cost of disposal
40	maintenance	Maintenance
30	Cost of	Lubrication
20	lubrication	Price
10	Price	

SOURCE   adapted from Snelgrove (2012)

There is evidence that some purchasing professionals still focus on price reduction. Recent research (Hesping and Schiele, 2015) reveals that even when focusing on additional value, purchasers will occasionally use transactional tactics with suppliers, and suppliers need to recognize when that is happening and get the discussion back on the track of long-term value. At a conference of professional buyers in Geneva, we established that less than 50 per cent were paid to win additional value for their organizations as opposed to being paid to get prices down. The encouraging fact to emerge, however, was that a big majority said that buying on value-in-use would be their preferred way of buying.

Price is always important and price discussions will never go away. After all, it is the easiest way for a customer to increase their profits at the supplier's expense. The purchaser will ask the question. It seems that many sales professionals are automatically provoked into negotiating mode when in reality there is no reason to be provoked. I was told early on in my career that the most important tool in a salesperson's toolbox is the word 'No'.

Contribution from an experienced key account manager

The disastrous consequences of buying only on price can be seen in the many huge government contracts, most of which have been a disaster and which subsequently cost the taxpayer dearly.

Value-driven purchasing can be good news for key account managers, but only if they know the account in detail, their sector, their operations, their customers and other stakeholders, and what they are trying to achieve (more on this in Chapter 5). Otherwise, it would be very difficult to express value in terms that purchasing professionals find at all interesting. First of all, it is vital to get a view about how the purchaser currently categorizes the value of the product category that you offer.

Value-driven purchasing can be good news for key account managers, but only if they know the account in detail, their sector, their operations, their customers and other stakeholders, and what they are trying to achieve.

The purchaser's matrix

Initially focused on direct materials and components, the reach of the procurement professional has extended into all aspects of corporate spend, from travel and stationery to IT software and professional services.

At the same time as this extension in the reach of procurement there has been a huge investment in people and systems. The modern procurement professional sits at the centre of an information web with almost limitless access to suppliers and prices.

The paradox is that they often know more about suppliers' prices and supplier markets than they do about their own business. Frequently, information on total cost of ownership, downtime, disruption, customer warranty claims and potential reputational damage is hard to come by and difficult to quantify. It is not unusual for a good key account manager to be better informed about the benefits of their product or solution than the procurement officer. Indeed, you would probably expect and hope this would be the case.

This presents a real dilemma for the sales community, which was described by George Akerlof in his Nobel prize-winning thesis: 'The market for "lemons": qualitative uncertainty and the market mechanism' (Akerlof, 1970). Akerlof demonstrated that in a buying decision where the purchaser has insufficient knowledge to quantify and accurately assess the additional value to be gained from a more expensive purchase the purchaser will reduce their risk of paying more than they should, by working on the premise that the safest thing to do is assume all products are more or less the same. Therefore, the prudent purchaser will buy at the average market price or lower, rather than take the risk of paying for something that cannot be proven or obtained.

Eventually, the higher-end suppliers understand that they cannot compete and reduce their offer to match or withdraw from the market. In the end the buyer loses. They get a cheaper but inferior product or service and innovation slowly dies.

So, here is the role of the modern key account manager – not to sell products or services to the purchaser but to inform and educate them to the point where they become an intelligent purchaser of value and not the manager of a price comparison process.

The modern purchaser has vast amounts of data on prices for similar products all claiming to be good enough. Why, then, would they take the risk to pay more in the hope that they will get a bigger prize, when the data on benefit realization is often scarce? The key account manager needs to derisk the purchasing decision by improving the purchaser's understanding of and trust in the positive outcome of a more expensive purchase.

Rob Maguire, Procurement Consultant and Partner of MaguireIzatt
(www.maguireizatt.co.uk)

Just as business developers in suppliers have analytics and matrices by which to judge the relative attractiveness of customers, it is only fair to recognize that the purchasing profession will be doing exactly the same thing. A long time ago, in 1983, Peter Kraljic designed a strategic sourcing matrix in response to concerns about the increasing risk in supply chains from globalization (see Figure 4.3). This matrix, or variations of it, is widely used in purchasing departments across the world for category management, and the *Harvard Business Review* article in which it appeared has been cited over 2,000 times (Kraljic, 1983).

Figure 4.3   Strategic sourcing matrix

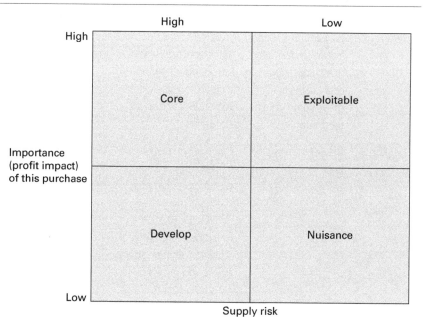

SOURCE adapted from Kraljic (1983)

Kraljic identified four categories of purchase, requiring different approaches (see Table 4.2):

- Where profit impact and supply risk are high, purchasers are willing to partner with the best supplier, who can be seen as *core* to their sourcing strategy.

- Where profit impact is low but there is supply risk, it makes sense to secure regular supply while waiting for conditions in the supply market to improve. Suppliers might be *developed*, but they might also be superseded when their differentiation is challenged, eg a patent runs out.

- Where profit impact is high and supply risk is low, there are multiple suppliers offering similar offerings and purchasers see the suppliers as *exploitable*. They can bargain on price.

- Where profit impact is low and supply risk is low, short-term deals can work, but the purchasing process will be seen as a *nuisance*.

Table 4.2 Matrix used for category management

Category Type	Potential Objectives	Potential Strategies	Other Considerations
Core	Secure future development projects and invest; accurate demand forecasting: sustain or incrementally grow volume with best supplier.	Through shared strategic planning, supply can be secured and opportunities to introduce innovation-thought co-design with supplier can be considered.	Consider the risks of becoming locked in to the best supplier. Manage risks or develop contingency plans for exit.
Develop	Secure current supply. Seek ways to reduce supply risk.	Offer volume deal in return for price reduction. Examine whether the need is over-specified and could be standardized. Consider shifting some risk to the supplier, eg servicization of the product in use.	Constant monitoring needed for change in supply risk, new sources of supply or substitutes.

(continued)

Table 4.2   *(Continued)*

Category Type	Potential Objectives	Potential Strategies	Other Considerations
Exploitable	Play suppliers off against each other for best deal.	In order to save transaction costs, some price advantage might be traded for long-term contracts or favourable payment schedules over time. Reward efficient suppliers with partnerships.	Be aware of new developments from suppliers that decommoditize this category.
Nuisance	Minimize transaction costs; maximize cash flow.	E-procurement and automation wherever possible. Bundling of sub-categories for efficient logistics.	Consider outsourcing or using suppliers to manage processes associated with nuisance purchases.

SOURCE adapted from Gelderman and Weele (2002)

See Gelderman and Weele (2002) in the reference list for further details on how the Kraljic matrix is used.

As we have mentioned before, with most generalized analysis tools, the criteria that make a purchase important or risky vary from company to company depending on which sector they are in, what size they are and what goals they wish to achieve in what time frame.

Responding to your categorization

Before any supplier can make the case for their offering to be seen as more valuable, the account manager must appreciate where the purchaser currently categorizes them. Purchasing managers are paid to be objective, to the point that they may receive bonuses for reducing purchasing costs. This is especially likely to be the case where purchasing has been outsourced to a purchasing consultant.

You will note that in the Kraljic matrix, the horizontal axis discusses supply risk. This is what buyers have to manage, and they are extremely aware of economic and technical risks, but they are also aware of professional and personal risk. Who wants to be the buyer who made a purchase that wrecked the company? Entrepreneurs may have an approach to risk that encompasses affordable losses when decisions are taken to change something. A purchasing manager is working with the company's money, and may have a very low threshold, if any, of 'affordable loss'.

Core

Strategic suppliers of core value are important to purchasing managers, but there will only be a few of them. Research tells us that buyers do not necessarily enjoy being tied into any supplier in the long term, so they are very cautious in selecting trustworthy partners. Those suppliers, however, who understand their customers' businesses well and the problems and issues they face, and who develop financially quantified value propositions based on their customers' needs, are the ones who thrive and prosper and who create sustainable shareholder value.

There are ways to deal with being in other boxes in the purchasing matrix.

Develop

If your offering is low impact, but there are supply risks, expect some developmental interest from the buyer. However, you have to improve the impact of your product, perhaps by bundling it with complementary offers or adding significant service elements that enable the customer to shift some risk to you.

Exploitable

If your product has a high-profit impact but there are small risks in supply (exploitable), then expect to be played off against your competitors, particularly on price. You will need to demonstrate something very innovatively different in order to gain preference, but that can be innovative payment terms or process efficiency.

Nuisance

Is there any hope if your offering is classified as 'nuisance'? Are you a stationery or cleaning products supplier, for example? Research suggests that if you want to gain some preference, then make it very easy for your customer to do business with you. An easy-to-use portal, electronic monitoring of usage patterns to prompt for replenishment of supplies, interpreting data to suggest ways for the company to use less paper and cleaning products to improve their carbon footprint – these will all appeal to the busy buyer.

Performance monitoring

Many key account managers are not selling new business, but are managing an account where there is an existing relationship. It is still important to monitor every aspect of the customer's business environment and needs in order to keep bringing interesting ideas to the buying decision-makers. Any purchasing department will have supplier or vendor comparisons and, in addition to everything mentioned above, the key account manager really needs to know what might be emerging on the purchasing manager's desk about comparative performance. A simple example is given in Table 4.3.

We can see in Table 4.3 that while we have an overall advantage, the devil is in the detail. Why is relationship quality so low? Think about the case of QG at the beginning of the chapter – when did the sales director last pick up the phone? What may be protecting us from the competition is a good score on 'ease of doing business' and the competitor's inability to deliver on time. What happens if they fix that?

It is fatal to allow any drift from superior performance on factors that matter to the customer. It is also fatal to question the customer's score. What they perceive is what they perceive. Numerous information technology contracts have foundered when the supplier produced plenty of data to prove that service-level agreements (SLAs) were being met, but the users of their equipment just did not feel that the 'spirit of the SLA' was observed. Cause of exit for suppliers include

Table 4.3 Comparative performance example

Success Factor	Weighting	Your Score	Your Weighted Score	Main Competitor Score	Main Competitor Weighted Score
Price	10	3	30	6	60
Delivery	10	8	80	4	40
Reliability	10	8	80	8	80
Ease of doing business	20	8	160	5	100
Relationship quality	10	3	30	6	60
Innovation	20	5	100	3	60
Value-in-use	20	8	160	8	160
	100		640		560

SOURCE adapted from McDonald and Rogers (1998)

complacency, communication breakdowns, change in key players, breach of trust and failing to offer new solutions in a timely manner.

Let's return to the case of QG. We can see that the customer's business has been taken for granted. Perhaps ZLK is no longer of strategic interest in QG and they can be allowed to lapse. More likely, the key account manager needs to pull off an amazing re-energization of the relationship and beat off the competition. He or she will need all the information and analysis they can get in order to start the process.

So what is the hapless key account manager of QG going to do for Heine? He may have read this chapter and worked out how many people might have an interest in the QG product/service category. He might have worked out that – oh dear, perhaps QG is in Heine's 'exploitable' box. First of all, he needs to get a platform with senior managers in QG very quickly and ask for their support. Then he needs to find out from his key account team how they interpret the needs of their contacts. He may need to have difficult conversations about the faults that Heine has highlighted. He may have to ask for some financial compensation for ZLK for past mistakes. Most importantly, he is going to have to get colleagues coming up with ideas that will appeal to a value-oriented purchasing manager. And he needs to get them costed. It is going to be a very frenetic three days. The alternative is even higher risk. Directors playing golf together could hardly rule out a full market-testing exercise between QG and their competitors.

Closing thoughts

In this chapter we have discussed the nature of buying, something that many key account managers know way too little about. We hope that you have put yourself in your customer's shoes and found out something interesting about how they perceive you as a supplier. In Chapter 5 we show how to analyse the needs of major customers. Even more importantly, we explain how to develop financially quantified value propositions.

Action list

Find out every job holder who has an interest in your product/service in the key account. Who is their contact in your company? Is that contact part of the key account team? Should that contact at least be on your distribution list?

Go and sit with the purchasing manager in your company. How does he/she do things? If he or she took a job with your key account, would they give you the time of day?

References

Akerlof, GA (1970) The market for 'lemons': qualitative uncertainty and the market mechanism, *Quarterly Journal of Economics*, **84** (3), pp 488–500

Blaskovic, J, Ferrer, A and Easton, S (2014) *Procurement-Powered Business Performance*, A. T. Kearney Assessment of Excellence in Procurement Study 2014 [Online] www.atkearney.com

Donati, M (2015) CIPS joins forces with Applegate, *Supply Management*, 25 September

Gelderman, CJ and Weele, AJ (2002) Strategic direction through purchasing portfolio management: a case study, *Journal of Supply Chain Management*, **38** (1), pp 30–37

Hesping, FH and Schiele, H (2015) Purchasing strategy development: a multi-level review, *Journal of Purchasing and Supply Management*, **21** (2), pp 138–50

Kraljic, P (1983) Purchasing must become supply management, *Harvard Business Review*, **61** (5), pp 109–17

Maguire, R (2017) Value selling: the crucial importance of access to decision-makers from the procurement perspective, in *Value First Then Price*, ed A Hinterhuber and TC Snelgrove, pp 123–37, Routledge, Abingdon

McDonald, M and Rogers, B (1998) *Key Account Management: Learning from supplier and customer perspectives*, Butterworth-Heinemann, Oxford

Murphy, WH and Li, N (2015) Government, company, and dyadic factors affecting key account management performance in China: propositions to provoke research, *Industrial Marketing Management*, **51**, pp 115–21

Reichheld, F and Markey, B (2011) *The Ultimate Question 2.0: How Net Promoter companies thrive in a customer driven world*, Harvard Business Review Press, Boston, Massachusetts

Snelgrove, T (2012) Value pricing when you understand your customers: total cost of ownership – past, present and future, *Journal of Revenue and Pricing Management*, **11** (1), pp 76–80

Key account plans

05

Conventionally, sales forces were deployed when services or products had been developed by a supplier organization. In complex service offerings, sales forces may be needed even before the solution exists. Sales professionals will be required to engage with customers to co-create the service, and then employ a concerted interaction capability to engage various functions across the supplier organization to deliver it.

Marcos-Cuevas *et al* (2016: 106)

We have seen in earlier chapters that the buying profession has made giant strides forward in sophistication during the past 30 years and we understand why they do not appreciate simplistic selling approaches. Product push is especially galling to buyers when they have already searched extensively for solutions to their problems and have already formulated their ideas about what kind of supplier they want to deal with. So, buyers today demand a much more sophisticated approach from their suppliers, and key account managers need to have strategic skills. Several research projects examining the performance of key account management (KAM) programmes emphasize the importance of key account plans that map how the capabilities of the company can create value for the key account.

Once again, let's look at a case study that helps to illustrate the theme of the chapter. This time, we follow it through each planning step.

CASE STUDY   Planning for HGD PLC

For a medium-sized player in a food category, such as Tasty Pies Ltd, getting any attention from a big retail customer is extremely difficult. Once a reasonable relationship has been established, the need for innovation and process integration becomes imperative. There is always someone else who can knock you off the shelves by making a better price offer. However, major retailers are followers of customer insight. They know that they too are vulnerable. Consumers are switching a lot of their buying online and, even on the high street, new retail models are squeezing traditional players. So, suppliers that can help retailers to maximize return from every last centimetre of shelf space will be most likely to earn longer-term agreements. It should be noted that HGD is clearly not a supermarket engaging in the dark side of retailer behaviour such as taking six months to pay and demanding post-hoc rebates. But the company is anxious about its market share and sustainable profitability, so it will not give Tasty Pies Ltd shelf space unless they can help them to achieve both.

Why do plans?

Boxer Mike Tyson is alleged to have said that everyone has a plan until they get hit. An alternative view is that of the scientist Louis Pasteur, who is attributed with the view that chance favours the prepared mind. Few would blunder into a two-week holiday without finding their passports, packing the right sort of clothing and checking their route. However, the amount of analysis done before visiting customers, let alone making major presentations to them about long-term value delivery, has often been inadequate. The authors are aware of a senior sales professional who did not even look at the website of a customer before making a visit, and was surprised when he was challenged about it. 'The gift of the gab' does not impress the purchasing decision-makers of the 21st century.

Purchasing professionals repeatedly complain about the lack of quality of people whom suppliers send to negotiate value with them, and chief among the complaints is their lack of knowledge about their business. It seems obvious that a supplier needs in-depth knowledge about a customer who is truly a key account, but major accounts and some mid-tier accounts with developmental potential might justify some research. A transactional business only requires a standard offer to be made that has relevance to a large segment of the market. However, we have observed smaller companies noticing some attractive brands buying from their portal and then wanting to connect to test the potential for more activity. Some research must be done before making that type of call.

> Individual key account plans appear to be of particular significance in driving customer satisfaction.
>
> Davies and Ryals (2014: 1191)

Starting to plan

Typically, a key account plan's summary page would signal clearly the importance of the customer, the quality of relationship and the key aspirations for the future, as demonstrated in Figure 5.1.

HGD is a regular customer with a high growth rate. Although the level of growth is expected to decrease over time, it is critical to increase account share during the high growth period in order to maximize the potential of this relationship. This situation, possibly 'major account' with the potential to transition to 'key', definitely justifies the time and resources for an in-depth key account plan.

So what can be done about this? Where will the resource come from to do all this homework? It is not unreasonable to assign some responsibility to marketing for scanning the business environment and what is happening to customers. Modern technology makes so many things possible, and internet software that 'crawls' for new mentions of the customer, combined with customer analytics, can provide masses of raw material in a relevant format. With the 'internet of things', operations can also play a role because sensors embedded in products can send prompts to customers and to engineers or

Figure 5.1 Key account plan summary page

Three-Year Account Plan for Customer HGD PLC			
Sector: Food retail			
Volume of business in past year: £250,000			
Volume of annual business by end of plan period: £800,000			
Current status		**Planned status**	
Relationship quality	Co-operative	Relationship quality	Interdependent
Account share	25%	Account share	65%
Customer growth rate	10% PA	Customer growth rate	4% pa
Length of contract	3 years	Length of contract	7 years
Profitability	15%	Profitability	15%
Contact map	16 connections	Contact map	35 connections
Short description of value to be co-created with account over this period:			
Why will this plan succeed?			
Key risks:			
Account plan prepared by: Harry Quinn		Date: xx/xx/xxxx	

SOURCE adapted from B Rogers teaching material, Portsmouth Business School

account managers when something is happening that needs intervention. Nevertheless, a key account manager must know about the key account, not just present what someone else has produced, so it is very important for them to have an active role in interpreting information for key account planning. Let's start with the bigger picture.

In-depth analysis of the key account

Key account managers are supposed to be 'boundary spanners' who can see things from the customer's point of view. To ensure that thinking is embedded, key account planning must start from the customer's point of view.

Sources of opportunities and threats

Key account managers are supposed to be 'boundary spanners' who can see things from the customer's point of view. To ensure that thinking is embedded, key account planning must start from the customer's point of view. What is happening in their business environment? It is from that business environment that change will come, and when customers have to change things they need to evaluate which suppliers can help them in that quest.

Of course, we could cobble up a simple SWOT (strengths, weaknesses, opportunities and threats) matrix. But if we have not really analysed what our customer's strengths, weaknesses, opportunities and threats are (and where they come from), they will perceive the shallowness of our plan as soon as they start asking questions about it.

Figure 5.2   External factors that affect the customer's business

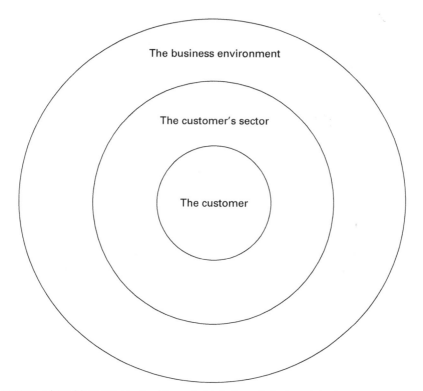

The business environment

The customer's sector

The customer

SOURCE adapted from B Rogers teaching material, Portsmouth Business School

Instead, we will compile an extended SWOT, and it will be much more insightful for some deep thinking behind it. Let us remember first of all that opportunities and threats come only from the external environment – the business context in which the customer operates, and factors in their industry sector (see Figure 5.2).

Many readers will have seen plans that start with a long list of environmental factors that affect life, the universe and everything. Obviously a key account plan should only feature factors particularly relevant to the customer. Nevertheless, we should not constrain our thinking too much in the early stages of the plan, otherwise some interesting factors can be missed. For example, higher education policy may not seem directly connected to food retail, but if raising student fees results in more young people staying at home during their university years, it will mean that the life cycle of the 'family shop' is extended for a large number of parents. Think creatively to begin with, and then subject the possibilities to a reality check.

Factors you are going to use in the plan need to be documented. Most organizations use an acronym to help with this process: PESTEL/STEEPL (political, economic, social, technological, environmental and legal) may be familiar. We condense this to PEST, since most legislation derives from policy, and much that is environmental feeds through into political, economic or social change (see Table 5.1). That might be reconsidered if the customer is in agriculture or fashion retail, as these sectors can be affected directly by weather patterns. However, let us continue with the example of our fast-growing food retailer.

At this stage, you may find it difficult to decide whether a PEST factor is a threat or an opportunity. To some extent, all change is threatening. You need to decide if it is the sort of change that the average retailer would welcome or not. It is the case that threats can be converted to opportunities. For example, if you can use your transparent, high-quality supply chain to differentiate yourself from competitors, then legislation about supply-chain fraud is not going to be a problem. We will examine these nuances when we get to the extended SWOT.

The next stage in the analysis of potential opportunities and threats affecting the customer is to look closely at their industry sector. In the 1980s, the Harvard strategist Michael Porter designed a technique for assessing the potential for profit in an industry sector. He called it the five forces (see Figure 5.3).

Table 5.1 Key account plan using PEST

The Business Environment for HGD

Factors:	Relevance to Food Consumption	Relevance to HGD	Degree of Effect in Next Three Years	Opportunity or Threat?
Political				
Measures to address supply-chain fraud in food industry	Consumer confidence in packaged food, eg lamb really is lamb	Need control and visibility of supply chain	High	Threat
Change in approach to planning law to protect town centres and local markets	Facilitates direct access to local food providers	More competition for top-up shops	Medium	Threat
Economic				
Possible change from food deflation to inflation	Food prices rise requiring change in spending habits	May need to change assortment and price promotions	High	Opportunity
Social				
More single elderly people as a proportion of the population	Growing segment needing easy packaging and small pack size	Work with suppliers for new ranges	High	Opportunity
Increase in special dietary requirements	Growing micro-segments for gluten-free, lactose-free, vegan, etc	Work with suppliers for new ranges	Medium	Opportunity

(continued)

Table 5.1 (*Continued*)

The Business Environment for HGD

	Relevance to Food Consumption	Relevance to HGD	Degree of Effect in Next Three Years	Opportunity or Threat?
Technology				
Sensors for stock control – in logistics, warehouse and on shelves	Technology-savvy customers expect special offers at the food shelf	Technology arms-race with competitors to maximize supply chain efficiency and customer responsiveness	High	Opportunity
Increased use of technology anytime, anywhere	Able to shop for anything from home or mobile device	As above, and need for time-specific 'click and collect' and home delivery	High	Threat

SOURCE adapted from Ryals and McDonald (2007)

Figure 5.3   Porter's five forces

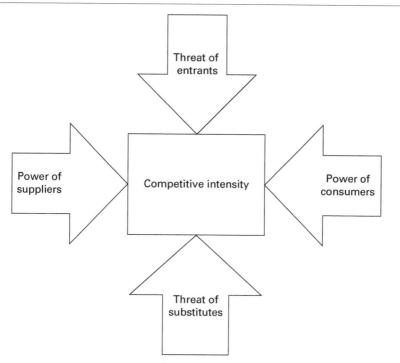

SOURCE adapted from Porter (1980)

Let's apply a simplified version to food retail (see Figure 5.4).

It looks like a very bleak prospect for our key account! The potential for profit is being squeezed from four out of the five forces. But our account is growing fast. So there must be some opportunities in this sector. We have to look a bit deeper (see Table 5.2). By concentrating only on power and on the immediate supply chain, this analysis does not go far enough.

Here are a few examples. It seems that there is relatively little use of power by suppliers, but there is a threat in the supply chain for a food scandal, such as the UK horsemeat scandal of 2013, and some retailers were affected more than others. There is intense competition, but the major players in food retail are undifferentiated, so differentiated retailers are less affected by this factor. Some food retailers tend to have relatively loyal customers.

Figure 5.4   Porter's five forces applied to food retail

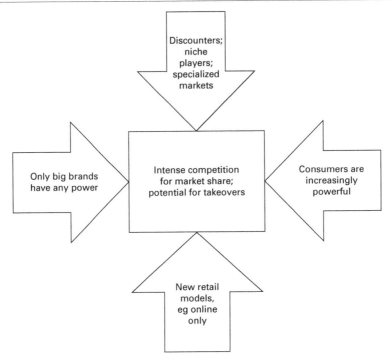

SOURCE adapted from Porter (1980)

Table 5.2   The competitive environment for HGD

	Relevance to HGD	Degree of Effect in Next Three Years	Opportunity or Threat?
Factors:			
Suppliers			
Limited power	Suppliers competing for business	Medium	Opportunity
Could be source of scandal	Supplier selection	High	Threat
Entrants			
Discounters	Price deflation	High	Threat
Markets	Limited	Low	
Substitutes			
Online models	Pressure to provide more online choice and delivery	High	Threat

(continued)

Table 5.2   *(Continued)*

	Relevance to HGD	Degree of Effect in Next Three Years	Opportunity or Threat?
Customers			
Increasing availability of information and power to choose	Pressure to provide more choice, flexibility and price competition	High	Threat
Intensity of competition			
Major players desperate for market share	Need to differentiate	High	Opportunity

SOURCE adapted from Ryals and McDonald (2007)

So, now we can summarize the sources of threats and opportunities for HGD. First of all, there is a theme emerging from both the PEST and five forces that consumers switching from shopping in shops to shopping online must be addressed. HGD must also be very vigilant in supply chain management and consider how to differentiate their offering and address emerging micro-segments. They must examine the potential for technology to improve operations and customer responsiveness.

Sources of strengths and weaknesses

How well equipped are HGD to meet these opportunities and threats? We need to look at their strengths and weaknesses. We can best do this by looking at their performance relative to competitors in the perceptions of the shopping public. There are usually plenty of market research reports that can help with such an analysis in most sectors. Let's look at the scores out of 10 that a sample of shoppers have given to a sample of food retailers including HGD (see Table 5.3).

Straight away we can see from Table 5.3 that our key account has clear strengths in food quality and store layout, and a clear weakness in the perception that shoppers have about their prices. The nearest

Table 5.3   Performance scores comparison across sample food retailers

Success Factor	HGD	Major A	Major B	Discounter	Niche
Price	3	5	6	9	3
Food quality	9	5	7	5	8
Choice in store	7	7	8	3	3
Choice online	5	7	6	0	0
Stock availability	8	6	4	5	8
Store layout	9	3	5	1	8
Brand you can trust	6	3	5	6	9

SOURCE adapted from B Rogers teaching material, Portsmouth Business School

competitor in terms of profile seems to be Major B. Looking at the bilateral comparison, another strength is stock availability, suggesting that HGD is fairly efficient. Relative weaknesses can be seen in the range of goods in store and online, and the trustworthiness of the brand is not as strong as we might expect.

The nine-box SWOT

Figure 5.5 shows an extended view of SWOT. We can see here the key account's objectives, which we should know, or should be able to find in their annual report. We can also see that there are things they need to do so that they can apply their strengths to opportunities and to diffuse threats. They need to invest to make sure that weaknesses do not neutralize opportunities, and defend situations where weaknesses are aligned with threats.

As the key account manager, we should be doing this thinking from the customer's point of view. We must postpone the delight of explaining where our products and services can help them achieve

Figure 5.5   An extended view of SWOT

Objectives Manage growth rate Increase market share to 10% Maintain operating profitability at 5%	Strengths Food quality Store ambience Stock availability	Weaknesses Price Range in store Range online Branding
Opportunities Micro-segments Major players undifferentiated	QUICK WINS	INVEST
Threats Consumer shift to online Supply chain scandal New technology for supply chain New technology for customer responsiveness	DIFFUSE	DEFEND

SOURCE adapted from Weihrich (1982)

Figure 5.6   Extended SWOT for HGD

Objectives Manage growth rate Increase market share to 10% Maintain operating profitability at 10%	Strengths Food quality Store ambience Stock availability	Weaknesses Price Range in store Range online Branding
Opportunities Micro-segments Major players undifferentiated	QUICK WINS Marketing messages about quality and the shopping experience Explore new ranges with suppliers that fit in with quality image	INVEST Explore new ranges with suppliers that fit in with quality image, but focused on micro-segments Invest in brand development
Threats Consumer shift to online Supply chain scandal New technology for supply chain New technology for customer responsiveness	DIFFUSE Use technology and supplier selection policies to ensure quality in supply chain Invest in IT to align online ambience with store ambience Ensure 'last mile' logistics as efficient as store logistics	DEFEND Defend price – it is the cost of quality Defend selectivity of choice – address multiple micro-segments rather than brand diversity Develop 'bricks and clicks' brand

SOURCE adapted from Weihrich (1982)

their objectives. Customers like account managers who understand their business in depth and bring them new ideas about how to succeed. So let's just do that. We may not like it in our personal lives when friends say 'If I were you, I would…', but in business we need and value critical friends. Of course, as the critical friend, we need to be diplomatic about having that conversation! Let's take a look at Figure 5.6 – the extended SWOT for HGD. This is the key account manager's analysis of what HGD should be planning.

The customer may not be able to do all these things at once. There has to be a conversation, hopefully at board level, about how the customer sees their business environment, what they are planning to do and how they are prioritising those strategies.

Then you can move to analysing how the value you have in your company's capabilities can be applied to the customer's needs. What does the nine-box SWOT for Tasty Pies Ltd look like, specific to this key account (see Figure 5.7)? Our opportunities and threats come

Figure 5.7   Extended SWOT for Tasty Pies Ltd to HGD (internal use)

Objectives Improve relationship quality from co-operative to interdependent Increase account share to 65% Maintain operating profitability at 15%	*Strengths* Quality ingredients Scores highly in taste tests Adaptability	*Weaknesses* Administration Logistics Branding
Opportunities HGD wants new ranges for singletons/elderly and micro-segments HGD wants quality assurance in supply chain	**QUICK WINS** New recipes and pack sizes for singletons/elderly Exchange more information regarding quality assurance	**INVEST** Willing to contribute to co-branding of niche products for micro-segments
Threats Increased expectations regarding use of IT in supply chain Expectations of support regarding online shopping Supplier investment in brand development	**DIFFUSE** Review implications of extending range into HGD's online range Willing to contribute to co-branding	**DEFEND** Potential to apply new technology and/or outsource and/or change supplier of failing functions

SOURCE adapted from Weihrich (1982)

exclusively from what HGD is trying to achieve, and our strengths and weaknesses are entirely determined by how the HGD key purchasing decision-makers see us compared to competitors. They may be doing very sophisticated supplier analysis and be willing to tell you the outcome. Or you may have to discern the strengths and weaknesses from their buying behaviour. If you have a small account share, it seems likely that you are perceived to be a comparatively weak or marginal supplier.

> *Our opportunities and threats come exclusively from what our key account is trying to achieve, and our strengths and weaknesses are entirely determined by how key purchasing decision-makers in our key account see us compared to competitors.*

Applying our competences to the customer's needs

When we switch back from the customers' shoes to our own, we do not necessarily share all our working papers, although we have nothing to hide. However, the first audience for our extended SWOT with HGD is colleagues in the account team. We have to have extensive discussions about the implications for new offers to the customer, how they can be resourced and our priorities – before we can complete our plan.

In sales, we generally like to be optimistic about what we can offer customers, especially key accounts. But our key accounts want us to be realistic. We may have great recipes for great pies, and be fairly adaptable to customer requests for new or different selections. Nevertheless, if we do not fix our administrative and logistical weaknesses at a time when our customer needs more technology-led efficiency, we will never be their preferred supplier. Obviously, decisions such as the outsourcing of administrative functions cannot be taken on the basis of one customer's expectations. So key account plans have to be collated and decisions made at a higher level. Some large companies have a sub-committee of the board that reviews key accounts monthly, so it is likely that trends affecting all key accounts, such as dissatisfaction with administration and logistics, would be picked up. If HGD is the only customer complaining about logistics, some separate courier arrangement might be necessary to reassure them. We call it 'papering over the cracks'. It comes with increased costs to serve the key account. As we have seen in previous chapters, increasing the costs to serve the key account might reduce its strategic attractiveness.

We can start to see the trade-offs that key account teams often have to make. It might be fairly easy to commit money to co-branding or promotional campaigns that the customer might like to run. Changing recipes and pack sizes takes considerable research and development, so the customer would have to give considerable assurances on future shelf space if a supplier of pies is going to invest, for example, in a gluten-free range.

Once key-account team members have debated the ways in which to offer value to the customer and come to a negotiated agreement that has board approval, the key account manager can make propositions to the customer. It is vital that the propositions have a very powerful resonance for the customer. As one chief executive we know used to say to his key account managers: 'Where's the spark?' For example, like Tasty Pies, all fast-moving consumer goods (FMCG) suppliers must give key accounts a compelling reason to trust them with a higher percentage of shelf space in a category. We believe that the best way to explain all of this and to develop value propositions for each key account is to take you through the process of arriving at financially quantified value propositions. Linking incremental spend with the delivery of cost savings is a compelling argument only if the buyer can have absolute confidence in your ability to deliver, or that you will share some risk.

> *It is vital that the propositions have a very powerful resonance for the customer. As one chief executive we know used to say to his key account managers: 'Where's the spark?'*

Identifying value-based projects

The hardest part of a KAM relationship is getting it started. Telling a customer that they are important to your business is tantamount to inviting them to ask for a discount. What is needed is a practical approach that interests the customer into collaborative working. One way to do this is for the key account manager to identify a value-based opportunity for the customer, and then propose a project to assess it. The word 'assess' is important here because it intentionally reduces the required customer commitment to that needed to agree to look at *the possibility*, rather than to act based on the suggestion. Where does the value-based opportunity come from? It comes from a detailed analysis of the customer's business and what they are trying to achieve with their customers. There are no shortcuts. A successful key account manager does their homework!

A project may start with a loose objective – for example, to look at how a new market could be exploited, or how a minor product modification may change the end customer's perception or cut manufacturing costs, and so on. Be prepared – between proposal and action, the customer may modify the project objectives. This is a good thing, as it shows thought and commitment by the customer.

Once the customer agrees about the benefits of the project, the key account manager should work with customer stakeholders to shape loose objectives into one or more specific, measurable, actionable and time-bounded goals. Note 'actionable' and 'time-bounded' as these are how a good key account manager moves the customer relationship forward. Actionable goals need people to action them and this provides the opportunity to introduce project team members from different functions, which further strengthens the supplier–customer relationship. Time-bounded provides a sense of urgency and priority to the project.

A well-run value-based project can open access to areas within the customer that are simply not open in commodity-based buyer–seller relationships. It has the twin benefits of providing information that will enable the KAM to identify better ways to build mutual value into the relationship and creating multiple, cross-functional relationships between supplier and customer. Over time, as the process is successfully repeated, the customer relationship will develop from exploratory to integrated KAM.

Phill McGowan, Chief Executive Officer of Positive Sales Limited
Phill has started B2B companies from scratch and developed them into medium-sized businesses, using relationship-selling approaches

Financially quantified value propositions

Value is essentially a simple concept – benefits minus costs versus the next best alternative. Value is not just created by a supplier and passed on to a customer; it can be collaboratively created between supplier, customers and other supply chain partners. Nevertheless, it is essential that key account managers start the process of creating value with their ideas about matching their employer's capabilities to their key account's needs.

A value proposition should be:

- **Distinctive:** it must be superior to competitors.
- **Measurable:** all value propositions should be based on tangible points of difference that can be quantified in monetary terms.
- **Sustainable:** it must have a significant life.

If these considerations are kept in mind, then you will craft meaningful value propositions. In the case of food retail, you need one for the consumer and one for the retailers.

Most sales professionals know that discounting is a losing game. It immediately erodes profitability and the organization's ability to sustain success. All companies have to keep their cost base low, within reason. We do not recommend industrial anorexia, where costs are constantly cut to the point of stripping so much value from products that customers do not want them any more. How often have retailers eroded their own brand with shoddy goods that have caused bad publicity?

It is worth noting that some customers only track cost savings in a particular fiscal period; next period they expect more. Typically it takes time to effect change (signed-off evidence for your reduced cost). The biggest gains are typically at the front end of your cost-saving initiative, which invariably diminish over time. Beware of contracting to incremental cost savings (year-on-year). They may be unachievable.

Paul Beaumont, Interim Sales Director

The alternative, of course, is meaningful differentiation. However, your differentiation is only really a marketing headline to your key accounts. 'Best quality ingredients' and 'best taste' position Tasty Pies Ltd versus their competitors, and hopefully marketing, research and development (R&D) and operations are working closely together to make sure that consumers always experience quality and taste when they buy the pies. But for the HGD category buyer, what does working more closely with Tasty mean? Let's look at some of the ways we can translate the nine-box SWOT into ideas for HGD, using another analysis that identifies the degree of value that HGD might perceive (see Figure 5.8).

Figure 5.8   Identifying perceived degree of value for HGD

Creating value For example, revenue gains, improved productivity, service enhancement, greater speed to market	**STRATEGIC** New recipes and pack sizes for singletons/elderly Extend Tasty range for online shopping	**HIGH POTENTIAL** Co-branded ranges in new micro-segments
Avoiding disadvantage For example, avoiding or reducing costs, avoiding or reducing risk, avoiding or reducing 'hassle'	**KEY OPERATIONAL** Use technology/third parties to improve process alignment	**SUPPORT** Exchange more information regarding quality assurance
	Operationally critical	**Non-critical**

SOURCE adapted from Ward and Peppard (2002)

The quadrants in the analysis shown in Figure 5.8 can be interpreted as follows:

- *Strategic*: something that will ensure the customer's long-term success.

- *High potential*: something that is worth piloting as it has potential for future value.

- *Key operational*: something critical to day-to-day business-as-usual operations – this could help the customer to avoid costs or risks.

- *Support*: something that provides a useful support function and could avoid some disadvantage.

Now comes the crucial question – so how much is the value worth to HGD? There are a number of ways of calculating value, as set out next.

Value chain analysis

Porter's concept of value added is an incremental one; he focuses on how an activity changes the value of goods and services as they pass through various stages of a value chain and within the internal value chain (see Table 5.4).

Table 5.4   Mapping value using Porter's internal value chain (example 1)

New Pack Sizes For Single Elderly					
	Impact	Added Value	Cost Reduction	Net Benefit	Notes
HGD value chain					
Inbound	Will be designed to fit current pallets	0	0	0	
Warehousing	Will be designed to suit current storage conditions	0	0	0	May require additional space
Distribution	Will be designed to fit current pallets	0	0	0	
In-store	Will be designed to fit in 'meal deal' and regular category display	0	0	0	May require additional promotional space end of aisle

(continued)

Table 5.4   *(Continued)*

New Pack Sizes For Single Elderly					
	Impact	Added Value	Cost Reduction	Net Benefit	Notes
HGD value chain					
Marketing and sales	Must conform to 'meal deals'	Increase sales of 'meal deals' by 2% October–March	0	2% x category turnover of average £2,000 per store per week for six months	Effect will be seasonal – more pies sold in winter
HGD infrastructure					
Finance	None	0	0	0	
Procurement	None	0	0	0	
Technology	None	0	0	0	
People	None	0	0	0	
Public image	May attract good publicity				

SOURCE adapted from M McDonald teaching material, Cranfield School of Management

Although in the example shown in Table 5.4 Tasty is not offering any cost advantage in HGD's value chain, doing the analysis shows that Tasty intends to be careful in its pack design *not to cause costs* by delivering packs that do not fit into existing plant. That is an important thing to demonstrate when introducing new ideas to customers, as it minimizes the risk of starting a pilot. It is likely that HGD would expect Tasty to contribute to offsetting the costs of any additional promotional space. The incremental income sounds marginal, and might not contribute to all that Tasty hopes to achieve with HGD, hence the need for a variety of ideas, and extensive research to back up claims.

If we remember the widgets example from Chapter 4, it can be seen that there is a much more extensive list of impacts on the customer's value chain that could be itemized and costed with that example (see Table 5.5).

Table 5.5 Mapping value using Porter's internal value chain (example 2)

New Widgets for the Jupiter Production Line (Annualized Benefits)					
	Impact	Added Value	Cost Reduction	Net Benefit	Notes
HGD value chain					
Inbound		0	0	0	
Operations	Fewer breakages	0	£100	£100	
	Less downtime		£1,000	£1,000	
	Less maintenance		£1,000	£1,000	
	Reduced lubrication		£5,000	£5,000	
Outbound	Reduced costs of disposal	0	£100	£100	
Marketing and sales	Contributes to continuity of supply	£2,000		£2,000	
HGD infrastructure					
Finance	None	0	0	0	
Procurement	Fewer transactions per year	0	£500	£500	
Technology	None	0	0	0	
People	None	0	0	0	
Public image					

SOURCE adapted from M McDonald teaching material, Cranfield School of Management

Shareholder value analysis (SVA)

Alfred Rappaport's (1983) research on shareholder value analysis (SVA) has been well received. It analyses how decisions affect the net present value of cash to shareholders. The analysis measures an activity's ability to earn more than its total cost of capital. SVA provides a framework for evaluating options for improving shareholder value by determining the trade-offs between reinvesting in existing activities, investing in new activities and returning cash to shareholders. We could simplify this to the scenarios of 'carry on as is', 'do something' or 'give up'.

Most companies today accept that financial targets in themselves are not the only possible business objectives. Measures of 'value added' such as brand equity, customer loyalty or customer satisfaction are reliable leading indicators to achieving financial results. However, in B2B sectors, financial decision-makers might treat a supplier's brand value as a risk-reducing factor, but not enough to generate value that means something to their customers. There are exceptions, such as having Rolls-Royce engines in aeroplanes and the chip-maker Intel's 'Intel Inside' campaigns with personal computer manufacturers.

When power plants are sold to utility companies, new production machinery is sold to manufacturers, or major IT systems resold to banks, it is highly likely that a full cash-flow and balance-sheet impact statement would be needed (some typical ratios are shown in Figure 5.9). For many incremental sales to key accounts, a simplified financial analysis of cash flow impact over time would suffice.

Whichever way you choose to illustrate the financial impact of your proposal, financial quantification will help you to increase profitable sales for a number of reasons:

- Consultants suggest that relatively few companies do financially quantified value propositions particularly well, so they may help you to be seen as more professional than competitors.

- Even if you do not have much differentiation, the very act of financially quantifying the benefits, even if they are standard benefits, may give you an advantage over your competitors.

- It should help you to reduce discounting.

Figure 5.9 Cash-flow and balance-sheet impact statement

Financial Analysis

Financial Ratio Indicator	Formula	Source			Company Standing	Industry Standing	Does it appear as though improvement is needed?		Are there any initial thoughts about how our organization's products/services can help?
		Annual Report					Yes	No	
Current Ratio	Current Assets / Current Liabilities								
Net Profit Margin	Net Profit / Net Sales								
Return on Assets	Net Profit / Total Assets								
Collection Period	Debtors Less Bad Debts / Average Day's sales								—
Stock Turnover	Cost of Goods Sold / Stock								

Description of Indicators		
Current Ratio	Measures the liquidity of a company – does it have enough money to pay the bills?
Net Profit Margin	Measures the overall profitability of a company by showing the percentage of sales retained as profit after taxes have been paid. If this ratio is acceptable, there probably is no need to calculate the Gross Profit or Operating Profit Margins
Return on Assets	Evaluates how effectively a company is managed by comparing the profitability of a company and its investments
Collection Period	Measures the activity of debtors. Prolonged collection period means that a company's funds are financing customers and not contributing to cash flow of the company
Stock Turnover	Evaluates how fast funds are flowing through Cost of Goods Sold to produce profit. If stock turns over faster, it is not in the plant as long before it is saleable as a product

SOURCE adapted from M McDonald teaching material, Cranfield School of Management

- It should help to make marketing campaigns more productive.
- In the case of smaller-scale sales over a portal, you might expect to see increased conversion of leads to sales in a shorter time scale.
- This kind of openness should improve customer relationships.

From strategy to action

Both the board and the customer will want to know how the fine ideas will be achieved. This is where it is vital for the account team to have, either permanently or for specific periods, an experienced project manager. He or she will probably use critical path analysis and sophisticated software to map and track what needs to happen for an idea to be implemented. For our purposes, a simple example of part of one element of an implementation plan is provided in Table 5.6.

Table 5.6 Element of an implementation table

Strategic Action	Items	Who	When
Investment in co-branding	Marketing manager to meet with customer and agency to explore ideas	JA to liaise with AW and GT on dates	Beg Y1Q1
	Agency to prepare creative and costings	GT (Agency)	End Y1Q1
	Preferred ideas to be approved by both boards	Harry Quinn to present	Beg Y1Q2
	Marketing teams to plan detail of media activity with agency. Involve operations and finance to ensure stock availability and cash flow	HQ to organize	ASAP after approval
	Pilot activity in selected stores	HGD merchandising supplier	Approval + six weeks
	Review and decision on scale of roll-out	All parties, HQ's PA to organize	Pilot + one week

Table 5.7 Contingency plans to overcome risk in marketing campaigns

Strategic Action	Risks	Contingency Plan
Investment in co-branding	Agency fail to fully test acceptability of creatives, and there are complaints about the advertisements	Ensure agency has back-up plan for withdrawal of material at any time. Pre-agreement on sharing costs of withdrawal
	Campaign generates more demand than anticipated	Pre-arrangements with operating staff regarding potential extension of shifts during the campaign period
	Campaign generates less demand than expected	Potential element of price promotion, which can be turned on mid-campaign; financial cover for reduced cash flow
	Competition react with price reductions and counter-campaign	Potential element of price promotion, which can be turned on mid-campaign; financial cover for reduced cash flow

All parties will also want to know the risks involved. In the case of a co-branded marketing campaign, the risks are fairly obvious, and contingency plans must be made to overcome them (see Table 5.7).

What else must go into a key account plan? There are things that the key account manager and key account team will need to plan that might be considered part of the operational progress of a business relationship. When will meetings take place? How will new connections be made between the two companies? When will the directors meet for strategic reviews? How much time needs to be spent on visits to the key account headquarters and individual stores? These might be notated in appendices, but they are necessary in order to avoid any omission or complacency about just how much effort needs to go into the development of a key account relationship.

Plans and proposals

Companies can spend a lot of money on producing proposals, and there are no prizes for coming second.

Close supplier–customer relationships enable the sharing of plans, but in many cases key account managers still have to produce formal proposals in response to specifications. The proposal will be judged against those of the competition before negotiations start. This is always the case when selling to the public sector, and in sectors closely serving the public sector, such as defence. Proposals should include everything that a key account plan should include:

- a demonstration of understanding the customer's needs;
- a confirmation that the outcomes that the customer intends to achieve have been understood;
- a value map – applying supplier capabilities to customer needs;
- a specific, costed solution, showing that the impact of the change generated by the solution on the customer's operations (over time) has been understood;
- an assessment of risk and a plan for risk management;
- a substantiation of the value the supplier can deliver, backed up by evidence (eg references).

Companies can spend a lot of money on producing proposals, and there are no prizes for coming second. They should over-resource the winnable bids and drop the less hopeful. An objective bid/no bid review should be held at a number of points in the early stages of the process. A proposal should be written clearly, without jargon, and be accessible to the variety of professionals who will read it. Technology allows innovation – proposals can be delivered with videos embedded (eg to demonstrate a machine in use at a customer plant) or with links to various independent information sources (but make sure that those links work).

Planning gets better as we do more of it, and proposals also benefit from continuous improvement. Whether won or lost, major bids should be reviewed and lessons learnt.

(Table 5.8 sets out the criteria for an excellent plan.)

Closing thoughts

We have seen how key account plans are crafted from an in-depth understanding of the key account and mapping our capabilities to their future needs. We have looked at examples of planning documents involving Tasty Pies Ltd and a retailer, HGD. As we write this, more and more technology is becoming available that could automate significant parts of the process. Nevertheless, it will still need human key account managers to think about what the data is indicating, and to have the creativity to use it to generate new futures for the key account and their own organization. Before moving on to Chapter 6, which discusses account-based marketing (ABM), we urge you to read the appendix to this chapter about learning how to create plans for key accounts using simulation software. Whatever plan we have for our key accounts, our competitors will have one too. Through simulation, we can anticipate competitor moves and try to neutralize them before they happen.

Action list

Set aside some time for reviewing your current key account, using Table 5.8.

Consider updating your templates and processes for account planning.

Table 5.8 KAM plan evaluation guidelines

Executive summary	Clear and focused.
	Contains all essential facts and points.
	Conclusions drawn: not just undigested 'stuff'.
	Joined-up thinking: logical progression from analysis to objectives to strategies and actions.
	Major business and market issues recognized and given appropriate level of focus.
Analyses	Need for change traced back to business environment.
	Market maps and value chains available.
	Factors accurately carried forward to the SWOTs and listed in the right places.
	Key account nine-box SWOT precedes value mapping.
	Key account's evaluation of us as a supplier informs our nine-box SWOT.
	Is the key account's competitive position and our competitive position realistic?
Objectives	Customer wallet is defined accurately.
	Objectives match analysis, including downturns.
Strategy	Clear, explicit and explained, especially customer value proposition.
	Answers 'Why us?'
	Not 'wish-list' of sales outcomes.
	Not simple actions.
	Consistent with analyses: origins are clear.
	Resources are realistic.
	More than 'business as usual'.
	Acknowledges importance of customer's customer.
	Acknowledges potential reaction from competitors.
Action	Does not run out of steam in six months.
	Identified 'big' actions, not just 'set up meeting' etc.
	Includes metrics.
	Risks evaluated and mitigation defined.

SOURCE adapted from McDonald *et al* (2000)

References

Davies, IA and Ryals, LJ (2014) The effectiveness of key account management practices, *Industrial Marketing Management*, **43** (7), pp 1182–94

Marcos-Cuevas, J, Nätti, S, Palo, T and Baumann, J (2016) Value co-creation practices and capabilities: sustained purposeful engagement across B2B systems, *Industrial Marketing Management*, **56** (7), pp 97–107

McDonald, M, Rogers, B and Woodburn, D (2000) *Key Customers: How to manage them profitably*, Butterworth-Heinemann, Oxford

Porter, ME (1980) *Competitive Strategy*, The Free Press, New York

Rappaport, A (1983) Corporate performance standards and shareholder value, *Journal of Business Strategy*, **3** (4), pp 28–38

Ryals, L and McDonald, M (2007) *Key Account Plans: The practitioners' guide to profitable planning*, Routledge, Abingdon

Ward, J and Peppard, J (2002) *Strategic Planning for Information Systems*, John Wiley & Sons, Chichester

Weihrich, H (1982) The TOWS matrix – a tool for situational analysis, *Long Range Planning*, **15** (2), pp 54–66

Appendix 5.1: Learning how to plan using an account management simulation

Edmund Bradford, Managing Director, Market2Win Ltd

There are some very useful tools and models to help develop a good account plan, but how well are they used? We have all seen even simple SWOT analyses done badly. Often account plans are treated like tax forms, with blank boxes to be filled in. The resulting plan may look complete but lacks sufficient insight and strategy. This, we would argue, is caused by a lack of understanding of the tools, and lack of training in how to use them properly. Many professions, such as pilots, hone their skills using simulations, and key account managers can also use a simulation to improve their account planning, as shown in Figure 5.10.

Have you ever played chess or checkers (draughts in Europe)? If you have, you will know that you will NOT do very well if you make up your moves as you go along. For example, in chess, you need to

Figure 5.10 What problems do simulations help to solve?

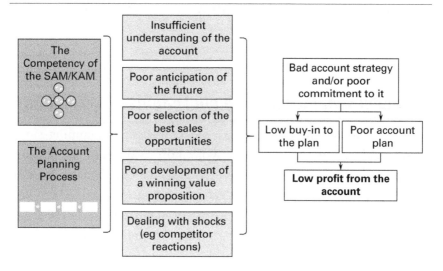

have a goal (such as capture the opponent's Queen) and a strategy (for example, box her into the corner and then remove her with one of the knights). The best chess players have a clear strategy converted into a clear set of actions *and* can anticipate their opponent's reactions to their decisions, many moves ahead.

Yet in the business world, where the stakes are much higher, companies are generally poor at anticipating their opponents' reactions to their account management decisions. As Coyne and Horn (2009) note: 'In chess we are told that the best players look ahead five or more moves... When asked the number of moves and countermoves they analysed, about 25 per cent of our respondents said that they modelled no interactions... Fewer than 10 per cent of the managers we surveyed looked at more than one round of response by more than one competitor.'

There is still a lot of inertia in account planning and implementation. Strategies are devised with scant thought given to how competitors will react to those strategies. It is as if competitors only exist on paper, have no influence on us or the marketplace, and our three-year account strategy will simply become a self-fulfilling prophecy. That is not realistic. The account plan needs to capture a strategy that is not only right but also *robust*. The strategy needs to be tested against likely reactions and scenarios that may occur over the planning period.

There is still a lot of inertia in account planning and implementation. Strategies are devised with scant thought given to how competitors will react to those strategies.

Example: simulation at a global engineering company

A global engineering company used a key account planning simulation (SAM2Win) in a two-day workshop to develop the account planning skills of its global account management staff. Five decision rounds were undertaken with great intensity and speed. There was also a specific session on using the procurement aspects of the simulation to learn how to align the supplier's selling strategy with the account's procurement strategy.

The workshop not only rapidly enhanced the participants' competencies in developing an account plan but it also provided a common language and understanding of what good account management looks like. At the end of the workshop, participants developed a personal action plan to apply their learning to their own accounts. One participant was pleased to say that she had already started segmenting her account on the back of an envelope before she left the room!

The core learning steps

In conducting a simulation, it is important to cover the following four steps in each decision round:

1 Review the situation that is being faced by the supplier.
2 Agree the account strategy that will improve the supplier's performance.
3 Update the account plan with the updated strategy.
4 Implement the strategy in the simulation.

These are illustrated in Figure 5.11, and it should be noted that two are done with the simulator software and two are done in the more traditional manner of discussion and writing a plan. Doing these four steps repeatedly over five decision rounds significantly improves the participants' ability to use the tools and templates correctly.

Figure 5.11   The advantage of simulations as a learning tool

These steps enhance knowledge, *skills* and behaviour

Observing/
Experimenting

Review
the
Situation

Doing/
Experiencing

Thinking/
Reflecting

Implement
the Plan

Agree the
Account
Strategy

Practise with a
Simulator

Update the
Account
Plan

Planning/
Concluding

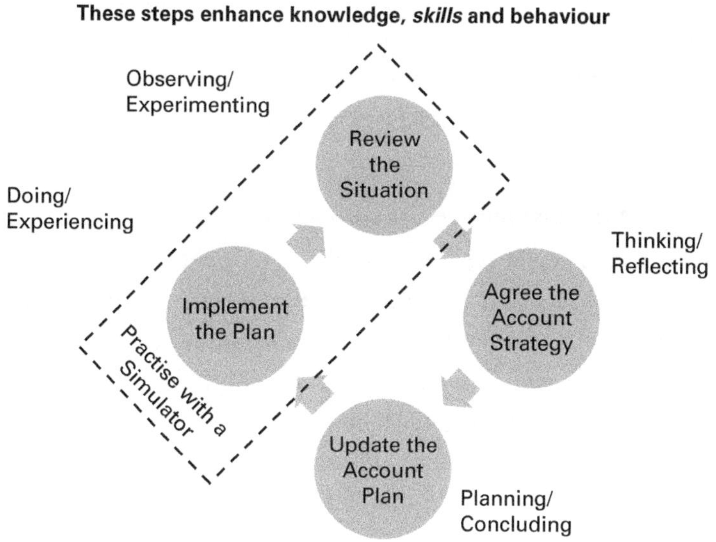

SOURCE: adapted from Kolb's learning cycle (Kolb, 1984)

The advantage of simulations as a learning tool

Academic and commercial research studies have identified a variety of advantages in using simulations to improve the speed with which the learners acquire skills and the degree to which they retain them. The learners can become immersed in the game, meaning that their learning is deeper, and they are motivated to improve their critical thinking, problem solving and decision making (see Loon *et al*, 2015). There is a basic human enjoyment in playing games. This ability to learn by play works for many different cultures and backgrounds from around the world. The competitive spirit kicks in and the desire to win drives the enthusiasm to learn new ideas that might give players an edge over their competitors. This is far more engaging than sitting through a dull presentation on an account and a list of all the projects we are doing there!

Increased innovation also develops from this cross-functional involvement in the simulation. Simulations have been used by many companies to develop new products and to develop collaborative innovation. The cost advantage is considerable, especially where large numbers of participants are involved. Simulations allow participants to meet online rather than physically, thus saving a large portion of the travel and meeting costs. From our experience, we would also add increased flexibility, greater competence, increased relevance and more practical outputs to the above list of benefits:

- *Increased flexibility*:
  Simulations can be undertaken either as concentrated workshops over, say, one to two days, or as online exercises conducted over several weeks (or a combination in a blended learning approach). In the latter case, this can fit around current job commitments quite easily. Participants may be given a week to make their decisions. They can share their thoughts about the market conditions and strategic options by e-mail, chat, telephone, webinar etc. They can be free to self-organize as best suits them – both in terms of their diary and their roles in the team.

- *Greater competence*:
  In order to develop competent strategic leaders, we need to develop their knowledge, skills and behaviour. Traditional training and development methods (such as seminars and workshops) are good at developing knowledge, okay at developing skills and poor at developing behaviour. This is because the participants learn the theory but do not have enough time to practise it. Like many other things in life, such as learning a musical instrument, learning a new language or becoming good at a chosen sport, practice makes perfect. It is understandable why so many account managers are poor at account strategy when they have not had the opportunity to practise it in a low-risk environment.

- *Increased relevance*:
  Because simulations can be tailored to the specific challenges of a business they are more relevant to the participants. For example, simulations can be tailored to product- or service-based businesses, specific industries, B2B and B2C, and to large or small companies.

- *More practical outputs*:
  This leads to our final point that simulations deliver more practical outputs. For example, good simulations can offer either a universal account plan template or allow clients to use their own templates. With a tailored simulation, participants can write their account management plans as they engage in the simulation. At the end of the exercise, they have a draft plan already written with the engaged input of many of the stakeholders who will be involved in its implementation. At the extreme end of this, real account plans can be 'war gamed' with one team playing the host and the other teams playing the competitors.

> Hours spent in an account management simulator builds good account managers, able to recognize threats quickly, respond to them correctly and implement the actions effectively and confidently.

Using account management simulations

Implementing an account strategy that has not been battle tested is like sending soldiers into battle with no back-up plan. Strategy is too important to be made up on the fly, lurching from one idea to another, panicking at competitor attacks and failing to hit account management targets because the market or account did not move as we expected.

Simulations help key account teams to practise how to develop and implement an account strategy. This means, rather than just selling more stuff, going back a step and asking whether we want to be selling that product in that sales opportunity at all. Is that opportunity important to us? Are there other products or services in other opportunities that are more important to us? What are the cross-selling opportunities? Even small businesses often sell multiple products or services into multiple customer areas. Often, the strategic account management issue for a business is not one of *zooming in* to the tactical detail of one product and selling it better, but more about *zooming out* to the total account and deciding where to focus the company's account management investment for the next few years. A good account management simulator will help the business take a truly strategic approach to their specific challenges.

Before we proceed, we offer a word of caution. Although we are using the term 'real' we actually mean 'realistic'. No simulation is going to model exactly the intricacies of your complex marketplace and your business. There are simply too many variables and too much irrational human behaviour. However, a study comparing some games to the Profit Impact of Marketing Strategies (PIMS) project administered by the Strategic Planning Institute (which has been analysing thousands of performance outcomes reported by real businesses since 1975 (http://pimsonline.com/about_pims_db.htm)) found that the games produced results consistent with PIMS, which seems to support the relevance of games and the standards that games producers endeavour to achieve (see Faria and Wellington, 2005).

In the same way that pilots use simulators to learn to fly, account managers can use simulators to learn to drive key account plans into action. Flight simulators model different landscapes and help pilots to deal with different scenarios, to make the right decisions swiftly and implement them effectively. The exact hazard that a pilot encounters in real life will probably differ from the simulated hazard. But the hours spent in the simulator builds the knowledge, skills and confidence needed in a good pilot. Similarly, the hours spent in an account management simulator builds good account managers, able to recognize threats quickly, respond to them correctly and implement the actions effectively and confidently. The resulting plan can then deserve the title of a strategic account plan.

For more information about SAM2Win go to www.sam2win.com.

Adapted by Edmund Bradford from E Bradford, S Erickson and
M McDonald (2012) *Marketing Navigation*, Goodfellow, Oxford,
ch 8, pp 206–16

Appendix 5.1 references

Coyne, KP and Horn, J (2009) Predicting your competitor's reaction, *Harvard Business Review*, **87** (4), pp 90–97

Faria, AJ and Wellington, WJ (2005) Validating business gaming: business game conformity with PIMS findings, *Simulation & Gaming*, **36** (2), pp 259–73

Kolb, DA (1984) *Experiential Learning: Experience as the source of learning and development*, Englewood Cliffs, Prentice Hall

Loon, M, Evans, J and Kerridge, C (2015) Learning with a strategic management simulation game: a case study, *The International Journal of Management Education*, **13** (3), pp 227–36

Understanding account-based marketing

Contributed by Bev Burgess, Senior Vice-President of ITSMA

> One of the biggest conversations in business-to-business (B2B) marketing today is the impact of account-based marketing (ABM). Spending on ABM is booming. For more than 20 years, **ITSMA** (Information Technology Services Marketing Association) has been innovating in B2B marketing services. In this chapter, we are delighted to welcome our guest contributor Bev Burgess, Senior Vice-President of ITSMA, who covers the essentials that everyone involved in growing accounts should know about this focused marketing technique.

A decade ago, defining account-based marketing (ABM) was easy. It was a relatively new strategic approach to create sustainable growth and profitability with a handful of a company's important clients, bringing the mindset, skills and resources of marketing to individual account teams. It was a collaborative approach that engaged sales, marketing, delivery and key executives towards achieving the client's business goals.

Today, based on the great success of the early adopters, as well as changes in the broader marketing and technology environment, ABM is suddenly being hyped as the next great revolution in B2B marketing. Vendors and pundits are making great claims about ABM transforming all of marketing. You have seen the headlines touting five simple steps to apply ABM to thousands of accounts and similarly silly slogans. Sure, ABM thinking and concepts can be applied to thousands of accounts, but there's a lot more to it than five simple steps!

The ABM excitement is coming from three directions:

1 The early adopters who have been implementing ABM with their key accounts, seeing results, and looking to expand and scale their ABM activities.

2 A conceptual shift in lead generation thinking from an individual to an account focus, fuelled by new technology to automate lead generation and tracking by account.

3 Marketing technology providers and agencies seeing new opportunities to sell technology, tools and services that complement recent trends such as contact intelligence, personalized content marketing and data analytics.

As the organization that pioneered ABM and that has helped develop and spread best practices since 2004, ITSMA couldn't be happier with all the attention. But one of the consequences of all the hype is growing confusion about what ABM is and isn't.

This chapter cuts through the noise with a clear definition of ABM and detailed descriptions of the three specific approaches that companies are taking. Robust, shared definitions ensure that all players – sales, marketing, delivery and other stakeholders – are working from the same operating manual. This is the first step to success with ABM.

Defining ABM

If you Google 'account-based marketing' you are bound to discover a variety of definitions, many confusing and contradictory. Each person or organization views ABM through its own lens – some with self-serving agendas to sell a particular technology platform or service. *ITSMA has penned this definition – Account-Based Marketing: treating individual accounts as markets in their own right.*

There are four underlying principles of ABM:

● **Client-centricity and insight.** With ABM, sales and marketing focus on solving the buyer's problem, rather than promoting the solution they want to sell. This outside-in approach means understanding clients and their organizations in enough depth to create propositions that help them achieve their business objectives.

- **Partnership between sales and marketing.** ABM will only achieve its potential when sales and marketing work hand in hand. This requires more than agreeing upon definitions, rules of engagement and a list of prioritized accounts. It means that sales and marketing are equal partners collaborating on the same team.

- **Focus on reputation and relationships, not just revenue.** ABM objectives focus on client lifetime value, going beyond lead generation and near-term revenue goals to drive increased mindshare and stronger, long-term relationships.

- **Tailored programmes and campaigns.** Using a combination of market insight, account insight and individual buyer insight, marketing and sales craft personalized content to drive interest and engagement.

Done right, ABM leads to significantly higher returns than any other marketing approach (see Figure 6.1).

Figure 6.1   How does ABM return on investment (ROI) compare to other marketing initiatives?

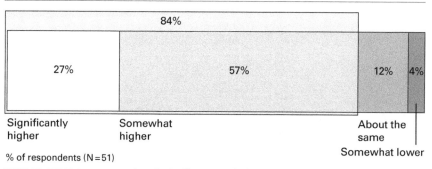

% of respondents (N = 51)

SOURCE ITSMA Account-Based Marketing℠ Survey, March 2016

In this context, it is not surprising that marketers want to achieve these results with more than a limited list of key accounts and apply the ABM approach across dozens, hundreds or even thousands of named accounts.

The three flavours of ABM

ABM is one of the hottest trends in B2B marketing for a very simple reason: it works. Some 78 per cent of B2B marketers say that ABM is very important or important to their marketing strategy,[1] and its importance continues to grow. ABM success is creating a virtuous cycle of increased internal demand (especially from sales teams) and investment. In 2016, 69 per cent of B2B marketers plan to increase their spending on ABM, according to ITSMA's most recent research.[2]

In response to the growing demand for ABM, as well as the growing recognition that lead generation and nurturing are more effective if managed and tracked in the context of a named account, companies have developed different approaches to enable faster programme expansion and broader coverage of accounts. Marketers are now implementing three different types of ABM: Strategic ABM, ABM Lite, and Programmatic ABM (see Figures 6.2 and 6.3).

Figure 6.2 The three flavours of ABM

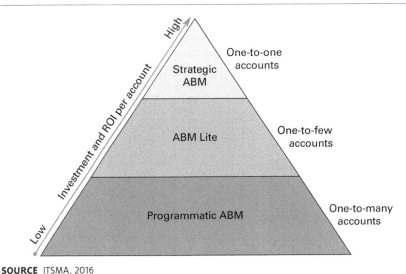

SOURCE ITSMA, 2016

Figure 6.3 The three flavours of ABM defined

	Strategic ABM	ABM Lite	Programmatic ABM
Definition	*Creating and executing highly customized programmes for individual accounts*	*Creating and executing lightly customized programmes for clusters of accounts with similar issues and needs*	*Leveraging technology to tailor marketing campaigns for specific named accounts at scale*
Marketer-to-account ratio	One-to-one (although a single marketer might be assigned more than one Strategic ABM account)	One-to-few	One-to-many
Average # accounts per full-time ABM-er	4	22	N/A
Account Focus	70% existing/30% new	56% existing/44% new	51% existing/49% new
Primary objectives	• Change perceptions • Build relationships • Identify opportunities	• Build relationships • Identify opportunities	• Generate leads
Nature of collaboration with sales	Integration with strategic account teams	Co-ordination with sales leadership and account teams	Co-ordination with sales leadership and sales operations
Source of Funding	Business unit, sales, marketing	Marketing	Marketing
Marketing content	Individualized, customized and repurposed	Customized and repurposed	Repurposed
Top tactics	• One-to-one meetings • Account-specific thought leadership • Innovation days • Executive engagement plans • Private events	• One-to-one meetings • E-mail marketing • Executive engagement plans • Custom collateral • Reverse IP/digital advertising	• E-mail marketing • One-to-one meetings • Reverse IP/digital advertising • Direct mail • Blogs/social engagement

SOURCE ITSMA, 2016

Strategic ABM: creating and executing highly customized marketing plans for individual accounts

This original ABM approach is usually reserved for strategic accounts and executed on a one-to-one basis. With Strategic ABM, account teams build stronger relationships with a company's most valued customers and prospects via highly targeted marketing interactions that demonstrate in-depth understanding of their business issues. Most importantly, Strategic ABM is done *with* clients, not *to* them, to drive value for both companies (see the Juniper case study – Appendix 6.1 at the end of this chapter).

With this approach, a dedicated, senior-level marketer works directly with one or a few strategic or key account teams on the sales side, and crafts fully customized marketing plans and programmes for each individual account as an integral part of the overall account plan. Technology can help with account insight, targeted communications and tracking progress, but the approach requires a significant amount of 'art' as well, including the creation of tailored value propositions, thought leadership and relationship development initiatives.

There is often a commitment to joint value creation via new offering development and innovation. Key metrics go well beyond revenue, to include brand perception, breadth and depth of relationships, new solution development, business collaboration and client advocacy.

Despite having the word 'marketing' in the name, Strategic ABM is not exclusively a marketing programme. Rather, it is a corporate initiative that directly impacts business outcomes such as revenue growth, advocacy and client lifetime value.

ABM Lite: creating and executing lightly customized programmes for clusters of accounts with similar issues and needs

This is a one-to-few model, typically applied to groups of strategic and/or second-tier named accounts. Companies already engaged in Strategic ABM often move to an ABM Lite approach to extend their initial success. Other companies start with ABM Lite to begin the transition to a more customized, account-based approach.

With ABM Lite, marketing programmes and campaigns are typically focused on small groups of accounts rather than individual accounts, usually 5–10 at a time that share similar business attributes, challenges and initiatives (eg tier-one retailers shifting to a personalized, omnichannel operating model).

Collaboration with sales is focused mainly on key decision points such as which accounts to target, which business issues to highlight, which propositions to promote, and how to tailor existing content for these one-to-few programmes and campaigns.

Technology can be more important with ABM Lite than with Strategic ABM, helping to automate the account insight process, campaign execution and measurement. The ABM Lite approach can cover more accounts with the same level of marketing resources, so is often attractive as companies want to scale beyond the smaller set of strategic accounts (see the Adobe case study – Appendix 6.2 at the end of this chapter). But the returns for any individual account will, of course, likely be 'lite' as well. Key metrics tracked are pipeline and revenue growth.

Programmatic ABM: leveraging technology to tailor marketing campaigns for specific named accounts at scale

This is the newest approach to ABM. With Programmatic ABM, marketing shifts its traditional focus from generating, nurturing and tracking leads by individual to an account-based view that better matches the account-based way that sales goes to market. Further, marketing uses the same account-based approach to support upselling, cross-selling, renewals and customer success.

This one-to-many approach is possible due to the latest technologies that enable razor-fine targeting, analytics and personalization across hundreds or even thousands of identified accounts. With an account-based view of the world, marketers can use Programmatic ABM tools to collect customer insight through social listening technologies, serve targeted content through reverse-IP recognition and cookies, and tie individual lead nurturing to overall account progress through the buy cycle.

With just one marketer working across hundreds of accounts, Programmatic ABM is much less marketing-resource intensive and can provide coverage far beyond Strategic ABM or ABM Lite.

Programmatic ABM can and should be aligned with the company's sales coverage model. Companies use Programmatic ABM to target specific segments (eg horizontal or vertical markets) or other groups of named accounts selected from across an overall market. They use outbound tactics to reach accounts on a named list, supplemented with inbound lead filtering to nurture those who are associated with the targeted accounts.

Key metrics include pipeline and revenue growth, as well as total revenue tied directly to ABM initiatives.

Which type of ABM is right for you?

Although some companies have been doing ABM for 10+ years, for most, it is still early days for the approach. The majority of companies in ITSMA's most recent ABM survey[2] have been practising ABM for two years or less and are in either the pilot or initial build stage of implementation. Some companies just do one type of ABM, usually Strategic ABM (see Figure 6.4). Some do a combination, most commonly Strategic ABM and ABM Lite. Increasingly, companies are exploring all three (see the Adobe case study – Appendix 6.2 at the end of this chapter).

The first decision for any business to make, once the three types of ABM are understood in the context of the company's wider go-to-market approach, is which type or combination of types will best support its business model and growth objectives:

- **Strategic ABM** is most appropriate for companies that sell high-value, sophisticated solutions. Moreover, it is best suited for top-tier accounts. These are the accounts that are so important that they can make or break the future business. Another way to look at this is customer lifetime value. The objective is either to grow your small share of a large wallet or to defend your already large share of that wallet. Strategic ABM only makes sense in accounts with large budgets because it is so resource intensive.

Figure 6.4   To date, few marketers have implemented all three types of ABM

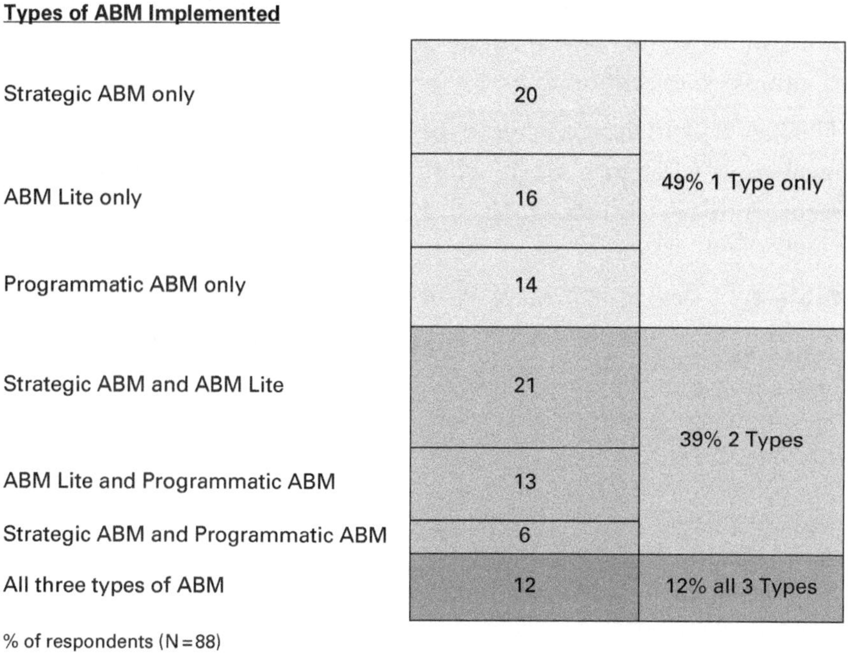

Types of ABM Implemented

Strategic ABM only	20	
ABM Lite only	16	49% 1 Type only
Programmatic ABM only	14	
Strategic ABM and ABM Lite	21	
ABM Lite and Programmatic ABM	13	39% 2 Types
Strategic ABM and Programmatic ABM	6	
All three types of ABM	12	12% all 3 Types

% of respondents (N = 88)

SOURCE ITSMA Account Based Marketing℠ Survey, March 2016
NOTE Differences are statistically significant

- **ABM Lite** is a good choice for companies that sell high-consideration, high-value solutions under two scenarios. First, targeted accounts are large and strategic, but the organization is unable to support the account teams on a one-to-one basis for a variety of reasons, most often due to resource or budget constraints or a lack of sales or senior management buy-in. Second, targeted accounts are characterized as second-tier accounts that, while still significant, do not warrant the investment of the top tier.

- **Programmatic ABM** is often reserved for accounts that do not yet warrant the individual investment of the other two types in companies with high-value, sophisticated solutions. In companies with lower-value sales that still want to adopt ABM principles to improve their campaign effectiveness, Programmatic ABM is usually the only form of ABM in practice.

  In companies with large deal sizes, programmatic ABM is often used to improve segment marketing (eg marketing to industries such as retail or healthcare) – or to mass-customize more horizontal marketing campaigns such as brand or offering campaigns. The same technology tools that are used for Programmatic ABM can also be used as tactical support for Strategic ABM and ABM Lite campaign execution.

The best way to decide which type or types of ABM are best for your business is to align with the company's sales and account management strategy (see Table 6.1).

Table 6.1   Aligning ABM with sales strategy

Sales Strategy	Ideal ABM Strategy	ABM Scaling Strategy
Account directors and teams allocated to strategic clients or prospects	Strategic ABM	ABM Lite
Account directors and teams handling multiple accounts at the same time	ABM Lite	Programmatic ABM
Sales coverage model across industries or geographies	Programmatic ABM	Segment or mass-customized marketing

SOURCE ITSMA, 2016

This alignment with your company's sales coverage model should go beyond ABM of course, into your wider go-to-market strategy, covering segment or industry marketing if you approach the market this way, as well as mass-customized marketing programmes such as your capability or brand programmes (see Figure 6.5).

Five misconceptions about ABM

With all the current hype about ABM, confusion and misconceptions are inevitable. Over the last 10 years, ITSMA has heard them all. So, just as we take the time to carefully explain what ABM *is*, we are equally committed to clarifying what ABM *is not*.

Misconception #1: ABM is just a marketing thing

It is important to stress that ABM is not just about doing marketing differently. ABM is not a marketing or sales tactic, or even

Figure 6.5   ABM in the context of your wider go-to-market strategy

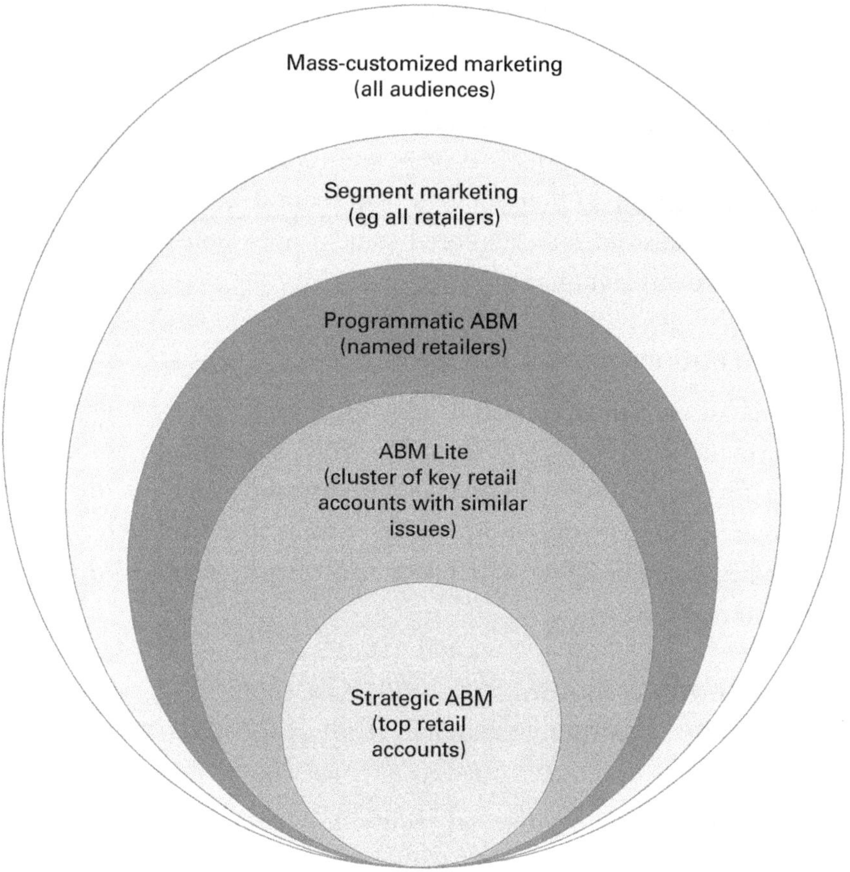

Mass-customized marketing
(all audiences)

Segment marketing
(eg all retailers)

Programmatic ABM
(named retailers)

ABM Lite
(cluster of key retail
accounts with similar
issues)

Strategic ABM
(top retail
accounts)

SOURCE ITSMA, 2016

a set of tactics; it is a *strategy* to build long-term relationships with the company's targeted accounts. ABM is a business change initiative to drive growth. It shifts the organizational focus from inside-out to outside-in, starting with the account and its problems and opportunities, and then working back to how the company can help.

Misconception #2: ABM can be done successfully without account intelligence

Account intelligence is what makes it 'account-based'. Otherwise, it is still 'spray and pray' marketing. Account intelligence positions you to:

- identify and proactively exploit new opportunities;

- enhance existing and build new senior-level account relationships;
- expand the scope and term of engagements;
- better align marketing and sales.

Primary and secondary research lies at the heart of ABM activity. You need to identify the business drivers and issues facing each account, cluster or segment so that you can map them to your own portfolio and develop customized or tailored value propositions, thought leadership and campaign plans.

Misconception #3: ABM is appropriate for every account

ABM is an investment and thus best used with those accounts that can provide a suitable ROI. As such, ABM is definitely not appropriate for all accounts. Further, suitability will vary by the ABM approach a company is taking. It is important to match each account to the best form of ABM, whether it be Strategic ABM, ABM Lite or Programmatic ABM.

Misconception #4: ABM is a standalone marketing programme – mutually exclusive from other marketing programmes

ABM does not stand alone. In reality, few ABM assets need to be entirely created from scratch. Collaboration with other groups to customize, personalize and adapt other programmes and assets is far more efficient, even with the most strategic accounts. Additionally, ABM accounts do not live in a vacuum. Chances are individuals at ABM accounts are going to be exposed to the outbound and inbound marketing programmes coming from other marketing groups across the company, whether they are industry marketing, product marketing or field marketing. Cross-marketing co-ordination is essential.

Misconception #5: Strategic ABM is another form of account planning

Strategic ABM does not replace, but rather facilitates, good account planning. Strategic ABM should be closely aligned with your key account management (hence the reason we are dedicating a chapter to it in this book). A key account plan, at its best, operates like a business plan, including objectives, sales targets, positioning, delivery and dependencies. But these plans often lack a specific marketing element.

Providing marketing expertise on account teams can help them to move beyond a narrow operational focus and spot potentially lucrative new opportunities. Marketing ensures the account teams have the right value propositions and the right content at the right time. Marketing provides insight to understand decision-makers and influencers, so sales can get them what they need to make the right decisions. Further, through Strategic ABM, marketing helps the account team to define priorities and identify the 'big bets' that they need in order to achieve their sales goals.

Getting everyone aligned

The best ABM programmes start by making sure that everyone really knows what ABM is, why you are investing in it and how it works. It is essential to take the time up front to cut through the confusion and hype, and make sure that all stakeholders involved in this important business growth initiative understand and agree on how the ABM process can support growth and other business objectives for existing and new accounts.

Beyond the ABM basics, marketing leaders and other stakeholders need to think hard about how best to apply ABM principles and approaches to their specific business model, market context and sales strategy. This may mean using more than one type of ABM; perhaps there is a place for all three types as marketing considers investments in different tiers of accounts to complement the investments being made by sales and business leaders.

Finally, once companies have decided which type or types of ABM fit best, they need to invest and maintain continuous focus on aligning marketing initiatives with account and overall sales management and processes. ABM is still a fairly new initiative for most companies. Once the early excitement passes, the hard work of ongoing collaboration across the company begins. To ensure the full benefits of ABM, it is essential to remain focused on the implementation of integrated programmes and campaigns across marketing and sales, while increasingly connecting with delivery and customer success programmes to accelerate growth and maximize the lifetime value of each account.

Appendix 6.1

CASE STUDY Juniper uses Strategic ABM to create mutual value[3]

Juniper's customer in this case study is a multinational provider of enterprise connectivity and IT services. The shift to a cloud first ecosystem and the emergence of new networking technologies based upon software-defined networking (SDN) and network function virtualization (NFV) was beginning to disrupt the provision of enterprise-focused networking solutions.

Furthermore, the market for the core product was forecast to decline due to price erosion and a saturation of the market. Recognizing the challenge facing the customer, Juniper identified its Cloud CPE (virtual customer premises equipment) solution as a perfect fit to help the customer respond to the business challenges it was facing.

The Cloud CPE opportunity was recognized as the single biggest long-term growth opportunity with the customer, and that it could lead to a step change in the volume of Juniper business. However, existing sales efforts were stuck within technical teams and were seen as being a 'science project'. The challenge was therefore to introduce a sense of urgency within the customer and accelerate time to market.

From the outset, Juniper recognized that this opportunity was different, as it required influencing a much wider range of stakeholders with the customer, many of them completely unknown to Juniper. Many of the new stakeholders were within the product management and marketing teams within the customer.

These stakeholders had different challenges to the traditional influencers in technology and operations.

It was decided that the ideal way to engage with these stakeholders was via the Service Creation Programme. This is centred around a series of workshops where the following ideas are addressed:

1   point of view on market trends and where the business value will arise from;

2   ideation of new services that are specifically tailored to the customer goals and existing business constraints;

3   business modelling of the value generated from the proposed new services;

4   go-to-market support for product definition, messaging and launch.

The unique approach of the Service Creation Programme is best summarized by a quote from another Juniper customer:

No other vendor has approached us with a similar model as Juniper. It really makes sense to analyse that space from a business perspective.

Vice-President of Business Development, Juniper customer

At the start of the campaign, a cross-functional team was brought together that included the sales team, the chief architect from Juniper for the account, the ABM lead and additional marketing experts from the corporate team. Working together, the key influencers were mapped out and scored based upon existing understanding of the Juniper solutions.

Through discussions with customers in the technology area, it was discovered that the product management teams had not identified the emerging need for a new service with the urgency that was required. Juniper framed the Service Creation Programme as a way to build consensus that the market was being disrupted and the customer needed to gain a sense of urgency to launch new solutions.

Juniper conducted a series of engagements with key stakeholders within the product management organization at the customer to build awareness and sell the idea of engaging in the Service Creation Programme via a series of workshops. Over a period of around six months, it was possible to build the consensus and then deliver a series of workshops.

Within these workshops, Juniper highlighted existing interoperability with other technology suppliers that needed to be part of the solution. Similar solutions being deployed by competitors to the customer were also referenced to illustrate that the market was already being disrupted and that the technology was mature enough to act now.

Following a successful series of workshops with the customer, they identified five new services that they would like to take to market. Four of the five services had the potential for a significant amount of Juniper technology within the solution. These services were then simplified in to a single new solution that combined many of them in a multi-vendor environment.

Juniper developed a demo of the new solution that was first shown to the client's CEO, before using it to influence other executives. The same demo is showcased by Juniper's customer at external events. The customer is currently in final evaluations of technology suppliers and is expected to launch a service to the market in the coming months.

Appendix 6.2

CASE STUDY   Adobe accelerates growth with ABM at scale[4]

In 2012, Adobe recognized that a digital transformation of the business landscape was going to impact how creatives, document managers, technologists and marketers worked together to deliver the best-possible customer experience: delivering timely, relevant information, via the right channel, at the ideal time, to the right person. To address this change and position Adobe as the best partner to make this goal possible for its customers, Adobe set a goal to transition its marketing and sales models from that of selling individual products to one of a customer-centric, ABM approach, dedicated to developing, selling and implementing fully integrated digital marketing-platforms solutions.

The objectives of the Adobe ABM programme included:

- *Bringing greater value to Adobe customers by providing solutions that empower them to work more efficiently, effectively and creatively; and by creating a community of peers that enhances their efforts through learning and networking.*

- *Increasing Adobe understanding of customers, anticipate their needs, and develop more efficient solutions and processes that address those needs, thereby increasing market share/increased sales.*

- *Introducing new products, ideas and processes that advance the field of digital marketing, at large.*

Adobe rolled out an ABM-based approach in 2013 to a targeted group, Adobe's Strategic Accounts. The programme required sweeping change, including: new vision and goals, reorganization to enable cross-departmental co-operation, extensive internal and external education, innovation teams to improve processes and practices, new metrics for reward, measuring success, and more.

At the core of Adobe's ABM approach was a customer-centric, cross-organizational, enterprise-wide team that was devoted to the customer's success. Teams included: product development, marketing and sales, systems integration, customer support and training groups, as well as financial and legal counsel. Adobe supported customers with a single account manager who was responsible for leveraging the combined efforts of all Adobe resources to maximize the success that the customer could achieve with Adobe solutions.

Adobe also engaged its Marketing Operations organization to revamp its data reporting to incorporate full data analysis, modelling and visualizations. With access to frequent, highly accurate and easy-to-evaluate feedback on sales and marketing efforts, Adobe could be far more strategic, nimble and successful in its ABM approach.

Adobe rolled out a full complement of 100+ marketing activities, ranging from one-to-one engagements, to one-to-few vehicles, to one-to-many programmes. These yielded greater understanding and helped establish valuable relationships between Adobe and its customers, as well as among members of the Strategic Accounts community.

Adobe was uniquely positioned in the industry to lead an ABM-based approach, given its breadth of products to assemble into integrated platform solutions. The programme execution emphasized:

- A commitment to customer-centric solutions (a focus on mutual success).

- Industry insight and vision (astute strategists and leaders).

- A willingness to move swiftly (strong course of action and aggressive goals).

- Realigning company resources and processes (solid implementation plan).

- Agility and flexibility (a workforce that embraced change and challenge).

- Monitoring and measuring the results (innovative analytics and rigorous reporting).

- A commitment to continuous improvement (benchmarking, testing, adjusting).

- Alignment with the company's mission (to offer solutions that empower everyone – from emerging artists to global brands – to bring digital creations to life and deliver them to the right person at the right moment for the best results).

From 2013 to 2016 Adobe achieved significant improvements in sales, market share and customer satisfaction:

- Solutions per customer 2013–15 saw a 20 per cent increase.

- Customer satisfaction improvement 2013–15 was 20 per cent.

- *Share of wallet 2013–15 up 30 per cent.*
- *Percentage of Top 20 Adobe deals 2015 (deal size) up 80 per cent.*
- *Retention/renewal rates 2015 up 90 per cent.*
- *Revenue growth from 2013 to 2015 of 1,400 per cent.*
- *Retention and renewal rates average at 90 per cent.*

Adobe's innovative marketing programme is being benchmarked and scaled in a roll-out to broader teams within Adobe, laying a foundation that will benefit Adobe colleagues and customers on a global basis for years to come. With its transition to a new business model, Adobe also raised the bar in the industry, introducing more customized, effective and efficient ways of doing business. In this manner, Adobe's efforts serve to advance the fields of digital marketing, digital media and digital communications.

Appendix 6.3

CASE STUDY   Accelerating growth with Strategic ABM at Fujitsu

Fujitsu lacked mindshare in the European media sector, so when one of the world's largest broadcasters signalled its intention to rethink its IT service provision, it represented both a huge opportunity and an enormous challenge.

The company's relationship with the broadcaster was minimal and restricted to technology teams. The broadcaster's executives lacked awareness of Fujitsu's brand, expertise and innovation in media. The challenge was to create an 'unmissable' story that could win mindshare and disrupt the existing relationship.

Starting from scratch, Fujitsu needed to build:

- *Insights – and intelligence for a holistic view of the broadcaster, building over 100 new contacts and understanding their roles.*
- *Messaging – aligning Fujitsu's value with the broadcaster's key digital themes.*
- *Communications – a suite of content, thought leadership and campaigns built specifically for the broadcaster and delivered through the most appropriate channels.*
- *Opportunities – accelerating immediate sales pursuits with bid marketing support.*

- And, most important, was building the team and ensuring that sales and marketing were working together.

By bringing an ABM approach to the challenge, Fujitsu was able to get 'under the skin' of the broadcaster in a rigorous way. Not just about market-sector knowledge or, indeed, organization-specific knowledge, ABM seeks to understand the individuals who really matter within the customer organization.

Fujitsu identified key decision-makers and decision-makers who took them beyond the technology and networks teams and into the C-suite and the all-important governance board that acted as an intermediary between the broadcaster and policymakers. There could be no strategic dialogue without first identifying key stakeholders and their needs.

They united the sales, marketing and account management teams behind a common set of objectives and a consistent story for the broadcaster. By understanding the customer context, marketing can better support sales by, for example, backing up on-the-ground conversations with social media activity.

Fujitsu defined longer-term strategic goals for the broadcaster and accelerated immediate sales opportunities by supporting the sales team's pre-bid and tender work for three major transformation projects.

As a result of the insights and messaging, the three tender responses were united by a common set of themes. This was backed by a visual design that mirrored the broadcaster's digital drive and reinforced Fujitsu's broader strategic message. Such an approach broke new ground.

Fujitsu then implemented a broader ABM strategy for the broadcaster. Through a combination of desk research, market analysis and internal account workshops, they undertook a deep dive into the broadcaster for a holistic view of its key functions, pain points and strategy.

Fujitsu's generic campaigns and communications were individualized to the customer and supported the messaging of the ABM campaign. They grew social engagement through campaigns across Twitter, LinkedIn and the company blog. This gave key members of the team a voice on the top-of-mind themes for the broadcaster, reinforcing their industry credentials.

In addition to digital communications, relevant industry events attended by the broadcaster's key personnel were identified and targeted. These events gave the Fujitsu team rare opportunities to meet the broadcaster's senior decision-makers and opened up the door for follow-up conversations. Hosting a talent event for apprentices and graduates helped underscore the broadcaster's and Fujitsu's shared brand values. Fujitsu supports the customer's corporate social responsibility (CSR) initiatives and has been highly engaged in providing technical support, as a business sponsor, to help deliver those initiatives.

The ABM campaign helped Fujitsu win a place on a Framework agreement with the customer and the company is now seen as a strategic supplier. Fujitsu has also been shortlisted on two further deals. And, from a position of not being known to the customer, they now have a great relationship and have regular C-level conversations. The success of this campaign is proof that when sales and marketing are aligned, great things can happen.

Notes

1 ITSMA is a leading source for insight, community and hands-on help for B2B marketers in the connected economy. For more than 20 years, ITSMA has brought together leading marketers, analysts, consultants and trainers to lead the way in marketing for B2B services and solutions. This chapter is based on ITSMA's update report 'Account-Based Marketing (Re)Defined'. More details at itsma.com.

2 ITSMA Account-Based Marketing[SM] Survey, March 2016.

3 This case study is based on Juniper's submission into ITSMA's 2016 Marketing Excellence Awards, for which they won the Diamond award in the ABM category.

4 This case study is based on Adobe's submission into ITSMA's 2016 Marketing Excellence Awards, for which they won the Gold award in the ABM category.

People and skills 07
for key account
management

The role of the key account manager spans functional boundaries across the business. Not only does the key account manager have to have an in-depth understanding of their customer, they need to have a thorough understanding of their own organization's processes and capabilities along with the full backing of their team in order to be able to make and deliver upon commitments on behalf of their organization. Skill sets for key account managers are different to those of other sales professionals. Due to the functional boundary-spanning nature of their role, designing appropriate and sufficiently extensive training and development programmes remains a challenge.

A central pillar underpinning the key account management (KAM) approach is that of trust; interorganization trust is fundamental to the sustainability of the relationship and is perhaps one of the key determinants of successful long-term outcomes. With trust being central to the long-term success of KAM, the supplier organization has to be fully aligned to supporting the key account manager. Delivery on commitments by the broader team is fundamental to the ability of the key account managers to fulfil their own promises on behalf of their employer.

Darren Bayley, Commercial Director, Dentsply Sirona

Large, mature businesses with mature key accounts went through an evolution in the 1980s and 1990s, retraining senior sales professionals who had historically been trained to approach selling on a deal-by-deal adversarial basis. The purchasing profession would claim that it was responsible for persuading suppliers that they really needed a more strategic approach to winning and keeping their customers. In the authors' research in the 1990s, which encompassed interviews with sales managers, key account managers and purchasing decision-makers, it was clear that there had been some kind of movement from transaction-based selling to relationship management, and the professionalization of purchasing had been a key factor.

Purchasing had been an administrative function serving technical decision-makers. For example, in the IT sector, suppliers wooed data processing managers who specified their brand choice to purchasing. Partly because markets were becoming globalized and new sources of supply emerged, which were cheaper but also presented new risks, and partly because of the successful lobbying of professional bodies such as the Chartered Institute of Purchasing and Supply – with their robust qualifications and thought leadership status, purchasing managers got the attention of boards of directors. They could deliver much-needed savings, but they needed more power to manage suppliers, such as strategic resources. We do not wish to disrespect the suppliers with foresight who initiated more strategic relationships with their customers, but many companies struggled to transition to partnership with key accounts. We should also not escape the irony that in the 21st century, there is concern that the power of purchasing professionals has become destructive. Lean supply chains should serve all the links in the chain. Fanatical pursuit of cost savings by the most powerful player in the chain can backfire. One big brand in aeronautics was so keen on screwing suppliers that those suppliers found ways to leapfrog their supposedly strategic key customer and sell directly to the airlines.

Here is a scenario from the bad old days, told from the perspective of the purchasing manager of a major manufacturing company:

CASE STUDY Purchasing transformation at Darnley plc

Darnley has only three core raw materials, and needs a consistent quantity and quality, delivered to a regular schedule. It may seem like not a lot to ask. The company is not a major corporate, but it keeps a sizeable town employed.

Darnley used to have three suppliers for one of these raw materials, and it just wasn't working. It is perceived as a commodity, but quality can vary slightly, enough to cause problems in the end product. They found that getting deliveries on time could be problematic. One of the suppliers had a lorry break down and did not bother to tell them. Of course, the operations manager was relying on that delivery being on time. Manufacturing down-time is hugely expensive. Purchasing Manager Joe Simms commented: 'No one seemed particularly interested in our product, our plant and our processes. Suppliers commoditized themselves by failing to offer any differential service.'

So Darnley decided to go out to tender for a sole sourcing arrangement. That is a huge risk. On the one hand it ought to ensure security of supply, but if something happens to that supplier, it is difficult to switch to someone else. Joe Simms built in a contingency plan for a small proportion to come from another source, just in case, but he felt that there must be a supplier who had contingency plans for supply issues that would reassure him. 'We asked for a professional partnership', Joe explained. 'The supplier could manage stock of their product in our plant and deliver when replenishment was needed. The supplier had to ensure a consistent grade of product. It is a raw material where prices fluctuate, so we wanted to set parameters to stabilize prices per year over three years. At first, it seemed like we were paying too much, but it balanced out over time. We wanted access to relevant technical contacts, as well as an account manager who was interested in our business. For example, we would like to reduce the emissions from this factory, and it will take co-operation from a variety of suppliers to help us to achieve that.'

Darnley went out to tender with these requirements. Three potential suppliers were shortlisted. Joe Simms perceived that 'only one of the "key account managers" could even understand what we were asking for'. That key account manager was from the supplier with the smallest part of Darnley's business. That supplier went from a few per cent to 90+ per cent of Darnley's spend. Of course, they had to make some long-term commitments in terms of money and people, but the pay-off was worth it to both supplier and customer.

However, the traffic is not all one way. One of our alumni commented recently that a strategically minded purchasing director he knew returned to an organization after a gap of several years, and expressed dismay that key suppliers were still being treated transactionally.

The emergence of the key account manager

One of the most persistent complaints of purchasing professionals in the 1990s, and still today, is that suppliers send them account managers who are not skilled enough to understand their business and what they are trying to achieve. Unfortunately, many were perceived as overpaid talking brochures and order-takers. Purchasers had expected that just as they had changed from a tactical to strategic profession, sales should do so too. They had professional qualifications such as Fellowship of the Chartered Institute of Purchasing and Supply, some had Master's degrees in supply chain management alongside their experience, and suppliers were sending them salespeople who had received training on the product range but knew little about how they were used. Some had been trained to ask intelligent questions, but that was becoming a waste of time as exchanges of information could easily be achieved over the internet.

So, major companies set out to train their salespeople in the skills of KAM, which included value mapping, business cases, partnership building and team leadership. A key account manager needed to earn credibility in the customer's organization from the factory floor to the boardroom. Reskilling current employees can take a long time, and cost a lot of money. Some salespeople embraced the new skill set with enthusiasm, some were sceptical, and some were keen but could not quite get it. That is no problem when a company has a wide portfolio of customers, and salespeople can be redeployed to non-key accounts where their particular skill set would be more applicable. Also, given that salesperson turnover is higher than most other professional functions, there was a chance to recruit the skills and attributes that key accounts were demanding. However, it is not easy to recruit to a person specification that is as complex as that for a key account manager. Table 7.1 illustrates the full expectations of this role.

Table 7.1 The 'ideal' key account manager

	BRAND AMBASSADOR: A personification of the brand values of the company	BOUNDARY SPANNER: Able to see things from different points of view	VALUE CREATOR: Initiates new opportunities for realizing benefits from supplier–customer partnership	IMPLEMENTER: Able to follow through from design to measurable results for supplier and customer
People skills	High-quality verbal and written communications	Networking within the customer and own organization; listening	Win–win negotiation; presentation	Leadership and influence
Thinking skills	Strategic, long-term view	Analysing from the customer's view, understanding the customer experience/'value-in-use'	Creating new ideas	Attention to detail
Technical skills	Fluency in online and mobile communication and information tools	Languages; value-mapping	Ability to design new solutions financial skills, eg costing	Project management; team resourcing
Subject knowledge	Industry knowledge	Knowledge of the customer and supply chain	Knowledge of company capabilities and how they can be applied	Ethical/legal awareness
Personal qualities	Credibility; integrity	Cross-cultural understanding; likeability	Creativity; flexibility	Resilience; persistence

SOURCE adapted from McDonald, Rogers and Woodburn (2000) and B Rogers teaching material

Because of the broad array of skills needed, development is an ongoing process for key account managers. It is the sort of profession that never stands still.

In our early research in the field, we asked purchasing decision-makers what was the most important skill or attribute of a key account manager. The answer was, overwhelmingly, integrity. When discussing this with key account managers, some have been offended to think that their customers do not recognize their integrity. It is not that customers automatically assume that key account managers might lack integrity, but key account managers need to demonstrate it consistently in little ways such as being on time for meetings, and in big ways such as securing special delivery arrangements for the key account. Sometimes, it is personal things that the customer decision-maker remembers, such as the key account manager driving through the night themselves to deliver a key part. Many key account managers have anecdotes about exceptional personal commitments they have made to customers, including meeting up with subsidiaries in war zones and negotiating with government departments for immediate release of parts from customs.

Subsequent research has suggested that the ability to understand the customer's strategy and operations – and apply the products, services and capabilities of their organization to help the customer to succeed – is the skill that distinguishes the best key account managers. This is often called 'co-creation of value', because it is necessary to involve the customer in that design process. This is by no means easy, but it is something that can be taught. More sophisticated KAM programmes will provide the tools and techniques to help with this.

Of course, the customer insists that they don't want 'to be sold to' – so the key account manager needs the skill to avoid conflict.

Steve Jackson, Business Development Manager for a global manufacturing and services company

Because of the broad array of skills needed, development is an ongoing process for key account managers. It is the sort of profession that never stands still. No one is born a perfect key account manager, and individuals require different development plans.

Appointing key account managers is often the first thing that companies did when they were transitioning to longer-term relationships with strategic customers, but the investment could not stop there. Customers were inclined to ask – what use is a great account manager if they have no authority in the rest of the organization? What use is a great account manager if they are papering over the crack of systems that don't work for us? So, the investment programme moved on to key account teams and infrastructure and process projects.

In our experience a KAM academy must take account management and sales training to the next level. The basic skills of negotiating, planning and managing relationships are a given. Key account managers driving extremely successful programmes have the edge because they think, plan, innovate and lead cross-functional teams, and they drive the strategic changes required for ongoing results year after year. Through the successful delivery of the KAM academy in today's markets, the key account manager becomes a chief executive in their own right, managing their own portfolio and directing resources to achieve strong partnerships with their customer base. This cannot be about just a series of classroom exercises, but a sustained programme of thinking and realistic interventions, educating and challenging these leaders to achieve the next level in their own careers and lives.

Liz Machtynger, Partner, Customer Essential

Key account teams

Not every business relationship requires the full portfolio of skills and attributes in one person. It is prudent for a key account to have a key account team. The way in which key account teams are organized varies from company to company. Companies such as fast-moving consumer goods (FMCG) suppliers, with major retail chains as customers, may have over 200 people who are directly involved in supporting one international account. Those people may work in merchandising, logistics, finance, research and development, project management, information systems, operations or marketing. In such a large operation, the global account manager is a conductor of a big orchestra. Managerial and leadership skills will eclipse the need for technical skills, which will be available from other members of the team.

Life is not necessarily easy for members of a key account team. Take the example of an accounts clerk in Spain working on a key account owned by the French subsidiary of a US company. The finance director of the company overall expects all accounts clerks to treat financial probity as their first duty of care to the company. The country manager of Spain wants the accounts clerk to make sure that the positive cash flow of the Spanish operations is his or her first priority. Along comes the key account manager, who wants an international deal for the French-owned key account, which involves extended credit terms in every country. The accounts clerk is expected to make this happen, despite competing imperatives. Even if the key account is offering an increase in shelf space in return, and the alternative is reduced shelf space, it is still hard to do. It is very difficult for an individual in a job to cope with 'role ambiguity', ie being asked to do things that can appear to be contradictory (see Figure 7.1). Because of this, it has been noted in research that 'team spirit' is extremely important in key account teams. It is hard for big companies to create a culture in which people in different time zones and different functions from different cultures can perceive themselves as part of an important co-operative mission on behalf of a strategic part of the business. But it has to be created in order to implement the business plan that has been agreed with the key account.

In a smaller company, teams to support key accounts can be very flexible. Although internecine rivalries can arise in very small organizations, it is usually the case that it is easier for employees in small companies to see the 'bigger picture' in any special project or

Figure 7.1   The accounts clerk's dilemma – three bosses, three conflicting objectives

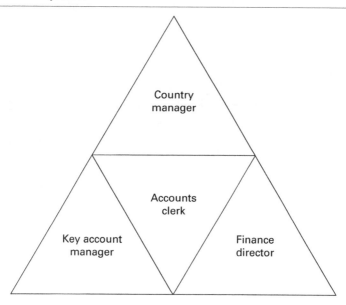

SOURCE adapted from B Rogers teaching material, Portsmouth Business School

relationship and overcome functional interests to support the overall company objectives. Communications are easier, and teams can be assembled and changed fairly quickly. Indeed, flexibility in the team membership can be advantageous as the customer's interests vary from time to time. It is important to make sure the right skill set is on a team, but attention must also be paid to team roles (see Table 7.2). The most important team support role in key account teams is the project manager, the person who makes sure that the account plan is implemented. The customer expects the key account manager to be an 'ideas person' – and that does not always sit well in an individual with 'getting things done'.

Our data indicates a significant positive association between top management involvement in KAM and success.

Workman, Homburg and Jenson (2003: 16)

Table 7.2 Key account team roles

Role	Description	Typical Function
Detective	Willing to go and get information and external ideas	R&D
Cheerleader	Helps the team to develop team spirit	Senior manager
Co-ordinator	Helps to allocate tasks	HR
Ideas person	Original and 'out of the box' thinker	Should be the key account manager
Critical friend	Logical person who makes sure team can deliver	Operations/finance
Specialist/s	In-depth knowledge of something currently relevant to the customer	Various
Driver	Provides energy to get things done	Various
Project manager	Takes the plan and works out how to implement it	Project management
Finisher	Attention to detail	Operations/finance

SOURCE adapted from Belbin (1993)

The reader will notice that a senior manager is a part of the typical key account team. This is something associated with success in several research studies. The senior manager devoting time to the team sends a clear message to the members of the team that it is an important part of the company, and it sends a clear message to the customer that they are strategic to this supplier. Researchers have actually tried to capture the amount of extra share of the account spend that can be attributed to the sponsorship of a senior executive in the account team, and it can be significantly positive. So there is a return on the investment in senior manager time. In large companies, we have observed a sub-committee of the board of directors that meets monthly with key account managers in addition to individual senior managers acting as board sponsors for particular customers.

If a board of directors recognizes that strategic customers are critical to the success of the company, then they do need to create the right culture in which KAM can be sustained. This means, not only talking the talk, but walking the talk. It also means signing up for a long-term programme of investments across the company, as illustrated in Figure 7.2. Each stage of the KAM evolution can take up to two years to complete. To implement wholesale change quickly requires even more investment and considerable risk. However, a smaller company taking on a global customer used to a KAM approach may find that the customer demands rapid evolution.

Figure 7.2   The evolution of KAM

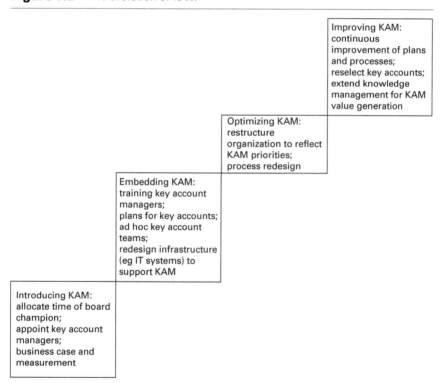

SOURCE adapted from Davies and Ryals (2009)

Resourcing decisions

As indicated in Figure 7.2, there are a lot of resourcing decisions to be made when implementing KAM. There is redeployment and process redesign. External help may often be needed to achieve these things. One of the biggest resourcing decisions is that concerning the role of the key account manager. Should it be someone redeployed? Should you recruit from the open market? Or could it be outsourced?

There are lots of advertisements for key account managers, with salaries and benefits varying enormously. It has been said that the key account manager of the most strategic customer is the next most important person in a company after the chief executive. Inevitably, the big brand names in the employer market command the most attention, and get the most applicants. It can be very difficult for smaller companies to compete. Professional selling skills, particularly for more senior roles, are in short supply. Even at the height of recession, government surveys find employers reporting difficulty in recruiting account managers. So what can be done? One medium-sized company in the pharmaceutical sector decided to engage a contract sales organization to find and employ key account managers on their behalf. Ultimately, in all resourcing decisions, senior managers must weigh up the pros and cons of developing a resource internally or buying it in from another organization.

It is particularly difficult to imagine outsourcing KAM. After all, strategic customers have such value to a supplier, and surely they would expect the supplier to employ someone directly to serve them. Certainly, reputational risk is a consideration in the decision, but it has to be weighed alongside other factors, as shown in Table 7.3.

Table 7.3 The stages of a make-or-buy decision at the customer interface

First Stage	Second Stage	Third Stage	Outcomes
Costs	Reputational risk	Supply market	Redeploy internally
			Recruit
Skills		Ability to manage	Partially outsource
			Full outsourcing
Flexibility			

SOURCE adapted from Rogers and Rodrigo (2015)

Decision-makers have to consider costs in any resourcing decision. Notably, in B2B sales, only cost leaders seem to treat it as the most heavily weighted factor. The skills needed to realize an opportunity are more important, and often lead to a preference for recruitment. Opportunities can be uncertain, so flexibility is also a first-stage consideration. Resourcing patterns may need to change quickly. The higher the risk, the more likely it is that redeployment and recruitment are likely to take too long and be too permanent, so short-term outsourcing might be used where flexibility is necessary.

As shown in Table 7.3, the next stage of the process is a consideration of reputational risk. Is this something that might undermine the customer relationship? Is it something that competitors do, or would we look less customer-centric in the market if we took this approach? Usually, suppliers perceive that employment is less risky than outsourcing, although the cost of a 'bad hire' can be considerable. There has been bad publicity for the outsourcing of selling and customer service in consumer markets. However, there are some very professional contract sales organizations in B2B and business-to-government markets.

The third stage introduces pragmatic factors that many companies find difficult to call. First of all, how can the supply markets be compared? It can be difficult to find good contract sales organizations in some sectors and some regions. It can also be costly and difficult to find good key account managers on the open recruitment market. Which is the lesser problem? Finally, how good are we at managing highly skilled professionals at the customer interface? Do we know how to treat them and to keep them? Salespeople often talk about leaving their manager rather than leaving their job. If there is little experience in the company in managing key account managers, or it would be too costly to develop it, perhaps it makes sense to let a specialist company take the strain. It is these two factors that often determine what a small to medium-sized company can do, and why some are choosing outsourcing. A key account manager employed by a contract sales organization can be dedicated to your brand and a good brand ambassador. A win–win compromise can be a 'temp view to perm' arrangement, whereby the contracted key account manager can eventually join the company on a permanent contract.

A key account manager employed by a contract sales organization can be dedicated to your brand and a good brand ambassador.

Recruitment, selection and on-boarding

In the case of KAM, the result of a resourcing decision is usually 'recruit'. There are good and less good ways to do it. Many companies put very restrictive statements in their advertisements, such as 'must have 10 years' experience of selling automatic gearboxes in the luxury car sector'. If you want to headhunt your direct competitor's account managers, it is prudent to use headhunters rather than advertise it. The cost of advertising is not justified when only a very few people are likely to fit the specification. However, beware wanting what your competitors have got. It creates 'groupthink' in the sector, so innovation is stifled. It undermines the diversity in the workforce that is associated with better company performance and corporate social responsibility. It encourages the sought-after clique of key account managers to be promiscuous between employers, creating a vortex of rising salary levels that are not justified.

It makes sense to be open-minded when looking for exceptional individuals. Not all key account managers come from a sales background. In manufacturing companies, engineers often transfer into KAM roles, but it is also possible for accountants, marketers and operational specialists to move into the role. It has been argued that it is hardest of all for a salesperson used to making transactional deals to become a key account manager, because the role requires such a broad spectrum of skills. For these individuals, the investment in training is significant as they need to develop a longer-term mindset and more thinking skills.

Advertising for key account managers

Advertisements should be accurate. Few ads talk about the long hours of negotiating internal politics to ensure a key account gets consistent terms of business across companies in the same group or across national boundaries. Ironically, customers value most highly the time that a key account manager spends within their own organization promoting customer interests. There is a correlation between a key account manager's internal network and their ability to deliver results with customers. So, if developing internal relationships is important, ads should not create the impression that the job is all about building a relationship with the customer.

Accuracy about the status of the company is also advisable. Applicants can look on websites such as Glassdoor and observe what current employees think about your terms and conditions and managerial quality, or they might use contacts on LinkedIn to make an assessment about a potential employer. Of course, employers can also search for a potential employee's online profile and compare it with their submitted CV.

Selecting key account managers

Selection is a two-way process. The employer should have a meaningful and fair approach to shortlisting, but the candidates will also come with some criteria for selecting a potential employer. In these days of multi-company, portfolio careers, professionals have personal brands. Is their personal brand a good fit with the company brand? That is part of the selection negotiation. Most senior appointments these days include scenario activities as well as interviews, and the scenarios can be far more revealing, especially when they include large numbers of people who can provide feedback on their evaluation of the candidates. If it is difficult or costly to create scenarios, there are online assessment centres that can be of some help. Psychometric tests are controversial, but may have a role. Research indicates that key account managers need to be extrovert, conscientious and friendly in order to maximize their success (Mahlamäki, Uusitalo and Mikkola, 2014), but this would be true in most roles that are customer-facing.

At all times in selection, be transparent and take detailed notes. Apart from the need to give sensible feedback to unsuccessful candidates, those notes may be useful in bringing the successful candidate on board.

On-boarding key account managers

> *To present a highly prized new member of staff with a dirty desk and their laptop still 'on order' on their first day is bound to make them wonder what they saw in the job.*

We are familiar with the expression 'buyer remorse' when a consumer has made a large purchase and suddenly realizes how much money they have handed over and how uncertain they are about the value of the product. The same can be observed in changing job. It is an accepted risk in recruitment that the star performer's current employer will make them a better offer when they hand in their notice. Senior jobs are turned down for many other reasons too, such as relocation of family proving too disruptive or the candidate not feeling quite right about their new colleagues, or even the key account itself. It is during the period between accepting an offer and starting a job that a candidate will feel nervous, even though they are also optimistic. Keeping in contact is important, and making sure that the preparation for their arrival is robust is absolutely critical. To present a highly prized new member of staff with a dirty desk and their laptop still 'on order' on their first day is bound to make them wonder what they saw in the job.

There is a huge amount of knowledge that new employees have to pick up in a short period of time and managers rarely have time to plan 'on-boarding' properly. Table 7.4 can be a useful guide.

The 'inform, welcome, guide' model was discovered by one of our alumni to be a useful one for mapping out how new key account managers acquire the knowledge they need in their first few weeks. A complication for a key account manager is that he or she needs to know all about their new employer *and* their new key account. Not surprisingly, while large employers tend to be organized to impart dry knowledge about policies and structures, the importance of someone feeling welcomed by colleagues and introduced to the informal side of the company is often overlooked. It is hugely important for someone to feel 'at home' as quickly as possible – it accelerates the on-boarding process and improves their productivity. In the case of

Table 7.4 Induction/on-boarding of a new key account manager

	INTERNAL			KEY ACCOUNT
	Inform	Welcome	Guide	Senior manager to brief the new person and introduce him/her to the customer
Cultural aspects of the company (jargon, history, myths, etc)		Imparted by colleagues at meetings, or socially		Informal discussions with key account team
Tasks	Job specification and briefing from manager		Feedback loops	Key account plan
Product/ service knowledge	Documents and training			Documents and training
Working relationships	Assignment of senior mentor	Introductions	Positive efforts to involve new person in projects	Handover from key account team/ main contact at customer
Social relationships		Opportunities for social interactions such as coffee breaks	Assignment of 'buddy' to help make connections	Facilitated by key member of account team or buddy
Politics			Normally imparted by mentor or buddy	Explained by key member of account team or buddy
Policies	Online training and briefings	Formal induction with HR/ other functions	Examples of application shared by workmates	Documents (in knowledge management system)

(continued)

Table 7.4   *(Continued)*

		INTERNAL		**KEY ACCOUNT**
Structure	Organization chart	Formal induction with HR/ other functions		Documents (in knowledge management system)
Performance criteria	Job specification and briefing from manager		Feedback loop	Account plan
Company objectives and strategy	Training/ briefings	Formal induction with HR/ other functions	Examples of application shared by workmates	Account plan

SOURCE adapted from Klein and Heuser (2008)

key account managers, being accepted by contacts at the customer is also critical to their intentions to stay. A change of key personnel is an occasion when customers may look around at alternative suppliers. They need to be reassured that the new person is even better than their predecessor.

The big picture

KAM has a large price tag. It is a business model that needs investment in people, infrastructure and processes, but the biggest of all is people.

Implementing a KAM programme involves a lot of change in organizations. When you have reached key milestones, the programme is probably ready for reconfiguration. We have returned to a number of themes in this narrative so far, and before we move on to internationalization, Table 7.5 provides a summary of all of the success factors in KAM programmes.

Table 7.5 Summary of success factors in KAM programmes

Strategy	Shared Values	Style	Systems	Staff	Skills
Develop concept of co-creation of value	Teamwork	Participative	Team performance targets and rewards (short term and long term)	Cross-functional teams	Idea generation
Long-term outlook for selected key accounts	Customer focus	Consultative	Cross-functional training and coaching	Senior management as members of teams and/or a key account sub-committee of the board	Financial acumen
Correct selection of key accounts	Innovation	Risk taking	Job flexibility		Strategy formulation
		Tolerance of failure			Industry knowledge
Allocation of resources to key accounts		Transformational	Market sensing and customer-specific research	Key account managers	Negotiation
		Learning			Presentation
Management of risk in key accounts			Customer profitability analysis		Communications
					Process mapping
Balance the customer portfolio			Account planning and budgeting		Supply network redesign
					Leadership
			Value analysis		Project management
					Ethics

SOURCE adapted from Guenzi and Storbacka (2015)

KAM has a large price tag. It is a business model that needs investment in people, infrastructure and processes, but the biggest of all is people. While existing staff adapt into account teams, the ever-increasing demands on the key account manager means that it is the role that will be most scrutinized by the employer and the customer. This chapter has outlined the nature of the role and how it can be filled. We have also discussed the composition of key account teams and how resourcing decisions should be made. We think things have moved on since the purchasing manager of Darnley complained that only one key account manager could understand what he wanted, but the bar keeps rising.

Action list

Review the make-up of your key account team. Are relevant roles covered? Who is the senior management sponsor? How could you improve their involvement?

Review how you make resourcing decisions. Are all factors taken into account?

Review your recruitment process – does it follow through into selection and on-boarding?

References

Belbin, RM (1993) *Team Roles at Work*, Butterworth-Heinemann, Oxford

Davies, IA and Ryals, LJ (2009) A stage model for transitioning to KAM, *Journal of Marketing Management*, 25 (9–10), pp 1027–48

Guenzi, P and Storbacka, K (2015) The organizational implications of implementing key account management: a case-based examination, *Industrial Marketing Management*, 45, pp 84–97

Klein, HJ and Heuser, AE (2008) The learning of socialization content: a framework for researching orientating practices, *Research in Personnel and Human Resources Management*, 27 (8), pp 279–336

Mahlamäki, T, Uusitalo, O and Mikkola, T (2014) The influence of personality on the job performance of strategic account managers, in *Handbook for Strategic Account Management*, ed D Woodburn and K Wilson, John Wiley & Sons Ltd, Chichester, pp 539–53

McDonald, M, Rogers, B and Woodburn, D (2000) *Key Customers: How to manage them profitably*, Butterworth-Heinemann, Oxford

Rogers, B and Rodrigo, P (2015) An exploratory study of factors influencing make-or-buy of sales activities: the perceptions of senior sales managers, *Strategic Outsourcing: An international journal*, **8** (2/3), pp 229–61

Workman, JP, Homburg, C and Jensen, O (2003) Intraorganizational determinants of key account management effectiveness, *Journal of the Academy of Marketing Science*, **31** (1), pp 3–21

Going global with key accounts 08

As part of the process of globalization, which began in the late 1980s, the big multinational enterprises started to demand support, and consistent pricing, across their global operations. Whilst these arrangements are often negotiated in a HQ environment, their implementation is often monstrously difficult for both the key account and the supplier organization. Aligning two multinational organizations at multiple levels (strategically, operationally and tactically) across multiple countries and continents is extraordinarily difficult, often financially challenging for the supplier and more often than not ends in failure. Those that do succeed in implementing global key account management (KAM) programmes successfully navigate a number of challenges. The global account initiative must be justified through the development of a robust business case in both the customer and supplier organizations. Many supplier organizations, including my own, have clear selection and threshold criteria that must be met before a key account will be considered for the investment needed for it to become a global account.

Simon Derbyshire, Vice-President, Capgemini Saudi Arabia
Capgemini: a global leader in consulting, technology and outsourcing services

The case study overleaf is typical of a movement some years ago by major manufacturing companies to concentrate resources on suppliers who could support their globalization strategy. As usual, there are some comments on the case study within the chapter and further comments at the end.

CASE STUDY IOQ Automotive Components Ltd

XYZ Autos AG has announced its plan to rationalize its product lines and supplier base. Worldwide, XYZ has 500,000 suppliers, and is targeting a reduction to 50,000 within five years. In short, suppliers will have to find a way of servicing them in every location in the world where they operate, and to a consistent standard. IOQ Automotive Components currently supplies XYZ in Germany, Belgium and the UK. IOQ has anticipated that partners could be found in more countries, but whether or not they could ensure that those partners service XYZ consistently is difficult to determine.

XYZ has agreed that smaller suppliers will need time to adjust. They have offered a three-year window to IOQ, who make parts for their popular European family car range. IOQ is a well-established company, but the prospect of a big global expansion based on one customer's demands is daunting. However, they know that other key accounts are likely to make similar demands. To fail to internationalize will result in IOQ's accessible market shrinking year on year.

The board have to make a decision – take on big investments and risks to keep key accounts, or stay small and retreat into niche markets.

In B2B, the customers most likely to be key accounts are also likely to be global in their scope, and to expect global scope from their suppliers.

Politicians urge businesses to trade internationally and government money is made available to provide support for exporting, which includes training and administrative support. For businesses started in smaller economies such as Ireland, Finland, New Zealand, Uruguay or Sri Lanka, the logic is obvious. There is no growth that is not international growth. The view is very different for businesses in hugely populous countries such as the United States and China, but nevertheless, in B2B sectors, the customers most likely to be key accounts are also likely to be global in their scope, and to expect global scope from their suppliers.

Traditional models of international market entry suggested that a company would saturate the accessible market share in its domestic market before venturing abroad. Exporting country by country would precede the setting up of long-term partnerships with local distributors or setting up subsidiaries. This has not been a relevant model since the dawn of the internet, where access to multiple export markets can be achieved in the very early life of a company. Many can celebrate being 'born global'. Both traditional and ultra-modern models are largely overlooked in discussion of KAM, where the cases examined are largely huge global suppliers partnered with huge global customers. In this book we are addressing a wider portfolio of scenarios, such as internet-only suppliers growing to a stage where they need to employ key account managers (such as Dell); companies having to expand internationally to keep a key account; and companies exporting to diversify their customer portfolio to reduce the risks inherent in over-reliance on key accounts.

Reasons to expand internationally

We are constantly being told that globalization is the new normal, but the challenges of doing business in geographically and culturally different markets can never be underestimated.

We are constantly being told that globalization is the new normal, but the challenges of doing business in geographically and culturally different markets can never be under-estimated. One of the most compelling reasons to go global is to meet the demands of a key account. In the period 1995–2005 many major companies rationalized their supplier base and marginalized or dropped suppliers who could only cover one country or region. Supplier rationalization is a constant threat and suppliers are often faced with the reality of supporting key accounts in all markets where they are present or none at all. Although that sounds uncomfortable, access to a key player in an overseas market is the main facilitator of international expansion, so key accounts may well feel that they are helping their suppliers to develop their businesses.

General macroeconomic trends such as the rapid development of previously inaccessible markets – for example, Romania and Vietnam –

together with the reduction of trade barriers, have driven the internationalization of most industry sectors. Even sub-categories of highly cultural products such as food and fashion are in high demand worldwide. Supply chain demands extend beyond key accounts. It may be that powerful upstream or downstream parts of the supply network in a particular sector require players to be present in particular locations, or at least to be able to service them. It seems unthinkable today that a serious communications hardware brand would not be operating in the Far East. Automotive parts manufacturers are usually operating across the main hubs of the sector in Germany, Japan and the United States. These trends have been very helpful to suppliers from small countries with limited local markets, and also to entrants into highly competitive local markets who need diversified customer portfolios.

The internal drive within small businesses to grow is also relevant. New ownership may bring new scope, new expectations, new alliances and new technical capabilities. Companies have a variety of resource options when they choose to expand, and whichever is chosen requires different skills to make sure that it is managed well to deliver a return.

With many customers now having global operations it is critical for any organization to be able to respond to their needs. Selling companies need to be able to accommodate their customers' preferences with regards to dealing with them at a global or local level or even somewhere in between. If both organizations are misaligned from this perspective, it becomes difficult to achieve true collaboration and partnership.

Emerging markets present a distinct challenge when it comes to adopting a KAM approach due to the dynamic nature of those markets. A number of factors influence this, including the 'war for talent'; higher levels of staff turnover affecting the sustainability of organizational capability in both supplier and customer organizations; and more uncertain financial conditions.

With the consolidation of purchasing accounts in many sectors, the key account manager needs to be able not only to navigate the decision-making unit to engage with the appropriate influencers and decision makers across functions – they also need to be able to speak their language in order to present a compelling proposition.

Darren Bayley, Commercial Director, Dentsply Sirona

Assessing strategies for internationalization

Figure 8.1 demonstrates the choices available to a company when a current key account requires international supply, or when the quest for key accounts goes global.

The vertical axis represents the ownership team's appetite for growth. Not all companies can or should go for growth at the expense of profitability or cash flow. It is not just Green activists who question the hunger for growth. The great strategist Michael Porter has questioned why stock markets love growth when profitability is much better for returns to shareholders. It is also questionable how much growth that companies report is actually real, ie 'organic' growth from within. Acquisitions look like growth in the short term, but often prove to erode shareholder value. Nevertheless, many entrepreneurs and management teams thrive on realizing opportunities faster than competitors. The benefit of taking a high risk is a high return, and if that risk can be managed then substantial rewards will follow.

Figure 8.1   Choices available for company internationalization

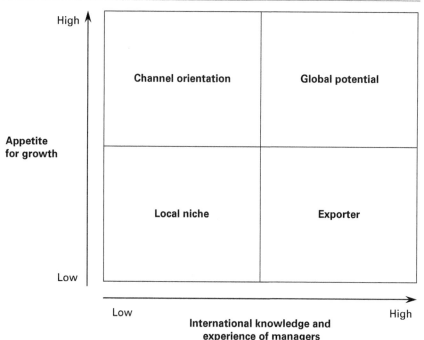

SOURCE adapted from Baum, Schwens and Kabst (2012)

The horizontal axis in Figure 8.1 represents the skills of the current management team. If a company wants to internationalize then skills have to be developed, recruited or bought in. It is not enough for these managers to just know about international markets. Many managers have lived and worked in other countries. Some countries have important social networks that are facilitators or inhibitors of business success, and managers with local experience might be in them. They should at least have some cross-cultural experience, which could be living abroad for some period of time, or studying abroad. Communications are more important than transactions alone. Managing relationship networks online is another aspect of success. Export, even within a key account relationship, generally starts with internet-based activity. Excellent technology that links easily into customer systems, supported by excellent communications, is associated with ease of internationalization and returns from it.

Leadership in the form of clear vision, commitment and communications are vital in addressing the significant change management challenges in both organizations. In the supplier organization this challenge manifests itself in a number of ways. For example, the local subsidiary organization will often have no engagement with the local subsidiary of the key account and may also not have the skills and resources locally to provide support even if they wanted to. Therefore, without investment and capability development in the local supplier organization (which should be part of the business case), it is often just not feasible for the local supplier organization to commit to supporting the key account. The local subsidiary of the key account will also often resist the implementation of global account management as it will be perceived as interference from HQ and will usually require the unpicking of local supplier relationships that have served the organization well for many years. Resolving these issues and creating the necessary alignment across many countries, time zones and cultures is both difficult and time consuming, requiring significant determination and resilience from those involved, not to mention a sizeable financial budget.

Simon Derbyshire, Vice-President, Capgemini Saudi Arabia
Capgemini: a global leader in consulting, technology and outsourcing services

Table 8.1 summarizes strategic approaches to internationalization from Figure 8.1.

Table 8.1   Strategic approaches to internationalization

Channel orientation	With an appetite for growth but limited knowledge, selective international expansion can be achieved with the help of sales agents in the chosen markets. However, there are two possible problems. Global accounts may not accept dealing with third parties, and prefer to partner with suppliers who have invested their own capital in the markets where they operate. If third-party brand ambassadors are accepted, the management of those third parties must be robust. Besides qualitative as well as quantitative objectives for the channel partner, there may have to be long-term arrangements in licensing agreements enabling a buy-out of the partner's local distribution rights when the supplier plans to have its own local presence, or compensation if the supplier chooses to exit the market. Original equipment manufacturers (OEMs) are always wary of the potential for partners to be opportunistic and to take commission for doing relatively little, or just to do very little. Channels have to be managed just as carefully as subsidiaries. If a supplier helps a distributor/agent to build their own business by investing in their marketing and sales skills, trust can be built up. Agents need to develop an internal motivation as much as employees. A key account will expect its suppliers' agents to provide consistent levels of service and brand ambassadorship. Business is business, but money is not enough for a long-term win–win.
Global potential	A combination of appetite for growth and managers with the right knowledge and experience to achieve it can be a powerful combination. Key accounts should feel reassured that wherever they are or will go, this type of supplier will be on board. How might that be done? Setting up subsidiaries might take a long time and swallow cash flow. Suitable acquisitions can also take time, and they will be expensive if the market is buoyant. They can be more difficult to manage than channel partners. However, a global player needs to avoid the 'virtuality trap' of having an internet-only presence in a market, unable to pick up the nuances of local market conditions and culture. A balanced portfolio of subsidiaries, acquisitions, agents and comprehensive local websites is possible, but different companies may decide to prefer a uniform business model that suits their culture and can even be a defining factor in their brand personality.

(continued)

Table 8.1   *(Continued)*

Local niche	Without an appetite for growth and managers with international experience, there is really no point in internationalizing with a key account. There are some cases where local niche product or service suppliers can do business with key accounts to serve a local market. Some food or fashion categories are only of interest in local markets, or particular legislative requirements in a country may require a global player to use local expertise.
Exporter	With a limited appetite for growth, but managers with skills in non-domestic markets, a company might benefit from tactical exporting to broaden its customer portfolio. It is acceptable to some global accounts to be served internationally from a base in one market. An obvious example is a food retail multinational buying Irish whiskey. Being based in Ireland would be an advantage in such a case. Parts for gearboxes are not so locally exclusive, but if a global account observes that a particular company has the best product, local manufacturing and export would be acceptable if the risks of supply interruption from a single source can be managed. Export can successfully be achieved with an internationalized website and working within e-marketplaces. Many categories of product are bought and sold internationally without much personal contact. The price of the product, the reliability of delivery and the quality of the product in use are all that the purchasing professionals want to know about. If repeat business becomes more complex, some relationship-building expertise will be needed.

SOURCE   adapted from Baum, Schwens and Kabst (2012)

From what little we know of the case-study company IOQ, channel orientation might be their preferred option.

What helps international growth?

If a key account wants to take a particular supplier into a new market, it is one of the best facilitators of international expansion, as automatically the supplier has a powerful reference site and a secure source of cash flow.

If a key account wants to take a particular supplier into a new market, it is one of the best facilitators of international expansion, as automatically the supplier has a powerful reference site and a secure source of cash flow. Of course, investments must be made to serve the key account's subsidiary in the new market, but they can also serve to offer extended geographic scope to other key accounts and to serve new prospects in the new market.

The next best facilitator of international growth is other kinds of supply chain links. Supply networks are very complex in many sectors. For example, in the information technology sector, if a key partner is planning to move into a new market, they may want to take with them established co-producers, service providers and sources of expertise.

Relational links

A great deal of business relies on personal networks. LinkedIn is a huge success because it enables businesspeople to stay in contact with all of their contacts. When people move jobs, they may wish to introduce the suppliers that they know and love to their new employers, and they may have moved to a company or business division in another country.

Rapid deployment to exclude competitors

> My mantra (inspired by the Special Air Service) is 'Speed, Ambition and Surprise'. A well-thought-out sales strategy implemented quickly, efficiently and effectively will gain the element of surprise enabling you to steal the march on any competitor.
>
> Paul Beaumont, Interim Sales Director

The first mover in a new market can gain sustainable competitive advantage. A supplier with a new product or significantly cheaper product may be contacted by potential customers from across the world and have to make choices about where local interest justifies investment. Contract sales organizations on relatively short-term contracts can be very helpful in building up a customer base in a new location quickly. Their use can also help suppliers to be flexible. If market conditions are difficult, the contract sales organization can continue to focus on its development. If the market conditions are favourable, the supplier can look for a local acquisition or use contractors to help to recruit local salespeople to set up an office.

Skills of key account managers

Operating internationally is not for the faint-hearted. As previously discussed, recruiting key account managers who at least have some cross-cultural awareness is essential. Extensive understanding of a new market's culture, including language, is even better. Although English seems to be everyone's second language, it would be really useful if some of us who have English as a first language could be proficient speakers of other languages. Larger companies often recruit key account managers close to the headquarters of major key accounts. If you were doing business with Siemens, it would help to understand the company if the key account manager were German, and equally an American would have a good cultural understanding of Wal-Mart. Companies must not cut across their legal obligations to ensure equal access to career opportunities, but a deep understanding of the national, ethnic, religious, social and business culture that influences specific key accounts is an important consideration when matching account managers to accounts. Where companies lack individuals with cross-cultural understanding, it would be prudent to work with contract sales organizations or sales agents who have it.

Flexibility

There is a financial concept called 'real options' that has been applied to international market entry. In short, it advocates the postponement of the commitment until uncertainty or risk in a particular investment has been reduced. Typically this is achieved through working with partners such as contract sales organizations who may be prepared to focus their activities on market entry, with a view to handing back customer relationships to their client when a sustainable market share has been established.

When a key account wants service in a new market, there can be no holding back on committing to an investment. However, identifying and working with third parties who can make the market entry smoother and faster is one way to reduce potential mistakes and losses. The key account may already have an established supply network and prefer new suppliers to fit into it. Relational skill and operational flexibility will help the transition.

What makes internationalization difficult?

> China's market development path and scale, Chinese culture and the Chinese state capitalism system create conditions that are distinctly China.
>
> Murphy and Li (2015: 116)

Starting as an internet-only company has its advantages in terms of cost management, and many powerful brands of the 21st century owe their success to their long-term commitment to e-channels in the 1990s. However, companies do not stay virtual forever. Some authors refer to a 'virtuality trap', because a deep understanding of the underlying drivers of markets and customers is difficult to achieve through impersonal electronic channels. Some internet-only players have achieved a level of attractiveness to major customers that requires investment in key account managers. Changing business model, or managing multiple business models, is a big decision for an organization, which may involve culture change and significant investments in people and fixed assets. The case for change must be compelling, well understood throughout the company and well implemented.

A deep understanding of the underlying drivers of markets and customers is difficult to achieve through impersonal electronic channels.

Local cultures – national, religious, ethnic, social and business

> People bring their cultural baggage with them wherever they go – and that includes the workplace.
>
> Jeanne Brett, professor of dispute resolution and negotiations (quoted in Knight, 2015)

Before the coming of the railway in the UK, people rarely travelled more than three miles from where they were born and travellers from the next village could be seen as alien. Throughout the 19th century these perceptions were overcome and national economies emerged. Easy international travel and the internet have facilitated global trade, but we are not yet a global village.

Relational links help international expansion and lack of them can make it very difficult. There are plenty of pages on the internet with examples of simple language problems making advertising slogans and brand names unworkable in some part of the world. For example, a car called 'Nova' may sound 'new' in English, but it is not going to be successful in Spain where 'No va' means 'it doesn't go'.

Where a global company supplies a global company, the key account team can consist of over 200 people from perhaps 40 different nationalities. We have noted that many professionals working in global corporations are willing to accept the company culture as over-riding their own local culture. For example, people who work for IBM often see themselves as IBMers first. Companies also encourage their cross-boundary account teams to develop their own team spirit or sub-culture within the overall business culture, and this can help the effectiveness of the team. This is not so easy to replicate in smaller companies or business networks, but thought should be given to the search for common ground for social discussion, such as sport.

Consider your own sense of belonging...

For example:

> Am I first and foremost English? Or part of a global community of sales
> professionals? Or a brand ambassador for my company's values? Or am
> I first and foremost a fan of Bolton Wanderers? Or am I proudest as a
> member of my extended family?

Readers may be familiar with the Chinese word '*Guanxi*' (a rough
anglicized pronunciation is 'Gwan-shee'). Guanxi, and similar
personal networks in Eastern cultures (see Table 8.2), are different
from personal networking in developed economies of the West, in
that the history of these concepts are rooted in times when survival
depended on exchange of favours from reliable friends and where
loyalty to the tribe or collective had to outweigh individualism.
Exchanges are personal, social and frequent, and obligations are not
time-limited. Western companies would find it difficult to engage
with these social networks and maintain the standards of transpar-
ency and objectivity expected by their legislators. The UK Bribery
Act forbids any distortion of trade. Connectivity is very important
in many business cultures, but care must be taken not to assume that
local networks work on the same principles as relationship marketing in the United States or the UK.

Table 8.2   Examples of culturally specific, informal social networks

China	Guanxi
Middle East	Wasta/Et moone
Thailand	Boon Koon
Russia	Blat
Japan	Kankei
Korea	Kwankye

*Focus on keeping the commercial promise – goods to a certain
specification and standard on a given date – is the first rule of trust
building, wherever you are in the world.*

In countries where specific relationship-building customs apply, researchers urge new exporters not to try to use them, as mistakes are inevitable and damaging. It is interesting to note that they suggest that a focus on keeping the commercial promise – goods to a certain specification and standard on a given date – is the first rule of trust building, wherever you are in the world. Nevertheless, some prudent preparation for meetings with international customers is advisable, and this should not be seen as a source of confusion or tension, but an opportunity for individuals and the company to learn. Here is a checklist of things to consider:

- What to wear – if in doubt, dress formally.

- Body language – gesticulation, eye contact, facial expressions, personal space required and sitting positions vary by culture. If in doubt, be conservative.

- Greetings – most cultures appreciate time being taken over greetings and introductions.

- Language – speaking clearly and in simple sentences, without jargon, is widely valued. It can be difficult and needs some practice. Think about the timing within conversations and the balance between speaking and listening. Giving the customer time to talk and an opportunity to demonstrate their understanding is very important. Equally, pause before answering their questions. It is a mark of respect in many cultures.

- Humour – avoid it until you really know someone.

- Concepts of time – 'now' and 'soon' mean different things in different cultures. Be specific when discussing time.

- Directness versus small talk – getting to the point is highly valued in some cultures and in others is considered very rude, but some relationship-building conversation is worth a try in all business encounters. Don't ask people things that you should have researched, eg their status. Assume people are higher status than might be obvious.

- Dealing with conflict – this is very difficult in any culture, but it has to be done. Proposing a win–win way out of problems is crucial.

- Teamwork and leadership – ideas about how to work in teams vary across cultures and a key account manager who has an international team needs to find out what team members expect. Treating people fairly and keeping them focused on the customer and company goals will tend to over-ride other ways in which team members belong.

First meetings are a platform for building goodwill. The core elements of any business relationship are contractual performance, competence and goodwill, but goodwill is necessary before contractual performance and competence can be demonstrated. Figure 8.2 is an overview of the main concepts involved.

Figure 8.2   Individual and corporate elements in building customer trust

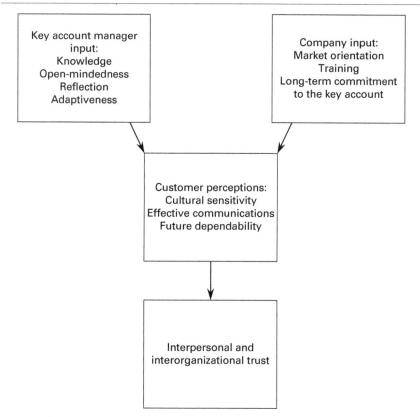

SOURCE adapted from Harich and LaBahn (1998)

In our case-study company, IOQ, the more culturally distant the subsidiaries of XYZ that they have to service, the more likely they are to need local third-party support.

Addressing differences in national culture is critical but is nearly always ducked or not addressed. This is one of those issues that fit into the '*too difficult*' box for many organizations, even those that are significantly multicultural in character. KAM has its origins in Western – and by that I mean the United States and Western Europe – business practices and was devised as one of the mechanisms used to operationalize relationship marketing as a response to globalization. It is, therefore, both a mirror and conceptualization of how business relationships are developed in this Western context. At its best KAM provides rich insight into the customer organization and serves as a value-creation platform for both organizations. At its worse it is a bureaucratic, formulaic, simplistic box-ticking exercise that adds little value. Outside of this Western context, however, it can be next to useless and even damaging to the process of relationship development.

In many countries outside of the West – including those in the Middle East, across Asia and the Indian subcontinent to those in the Far East – the nature and structure of society is profoundly different. Relationship development and its obligations, rights and duties are complex and alien to Westerners. In many of these societies there is no discernible distinction between personal/social relationships and business relationships. It is almost inconceivable that one could exist without the other, and a personal or social relationship is often a prerequisite for the development of a business relationship. This tightly woven social fabric is recognized by different names in different countries: in China it is called '*Guanxi*'; across the Middle East '*Wasta*' or '*Et-moone*'; in Thailand '*Boon Koon*'; in the Asian parts of Russia it is referred to as '*Blat*': all of which are characterized by deep social bonds, creation of psychological contracts together with distinct rights and duties and other obligations between friends and business partners. In the West these social processes are often looked on with suspicion and dismissed as nepotistic and even corrupt, but this is a grossly simplistic reaction borne out of ignorance and therefore becomes a missed opportunity in bridging this divide. The most successful Western organizations find a means of adapting to these cultural differences without compromising good ethical business practices, because the business value of doing so can be considerable.

I once described to a Saudi colleague the concepts of KAM. He thought it was funny that we needed a process, templates, spreadsheets and IT systems to build relationships with customers – he asked, '*Why don't you just talk to him, and understand his pains?*'

The issues discussed above often manifest themselves in the relationship between the headquarter organization of the supplier multinational company and the local subsidiary companies that are often landed with the task of making KAM work in a global context. Many large multinational companies derive their competitive advantage through their global, standardized and industrialized business processes, without which their organizations would descend into chaos. Their willingness and desire to adapt these processes to reflect local markets or cultural needs is often nil, because once you start to adapt to local needs these processes cease to be standard – and competitive advantage is lost and chaos is just around the corner. For the local subsidiary company this can be demotivational, as they know that what they are being asked to do is largely a waste of time in their context. The answer to this conundrum is often to create a hybrid model that satisfies head office but that also works locally. As long as both processes are transparent, and the relationship between them is clear, this can form the basis of an elegant model.

Simon Derbyshire, Vice-President of Capgemini Saudi Arabia
Capgemini: a global leader in consulting, technology and outsourcing services

Partner opportunism

Relationship building is one approach to reducing risks when trading in unfamiliar markets, and of course it is a key element of KAM. One of the impediments to any type of business relationship is a preconception common in economics and law that it is in the interest of parties in an agreement to shirk from their duties or to be opportunistic in seeking their own advantage at the expense of the other party. Contracts exist to stop this happening. But if a contract has to be enforced, trust has already been broken and damage has been done.

Every country has its share of quasi-criminal organizations posing as legitimate companies. Normally, they target vulnerable consumers, but optimistic smaller companies might also be on their radar. In some developing economies, exporting companies are concerned about piracy of their intellectual property or other breaches of confidentiality. If your new international partner is a subsidiary of an existing key account, this is unlikely to be the case. Even if it is a potential new agent to serve a key account in a new territory, the key account might be helpful in finding a suitable company. In other situations, trade associations and government departments can be helpful in suggesting ways of finding reputable partners. Opportunism is a risk that always has to be acknowledged and managed. The risk is obviously higher in unfamiliar markets and legal systems.

> A centralized group purchasing strategy is not a guarantee that every division/site worldwide is actually following the same strategy. I once secured a 'Europe-wide' contract from one of the world's leading brands. However, each site (of over 100) had its own maintenance budget; and group purchasing could not dictate how they spent it. In essence, group policy was only a set of guiding principles. You certainly don't want to be setting up group price plans in this sort of situation. Ask about the scope of agreements and whether central purchasing's view is mandatory or optional.
>
> Example from an experienced key account manager

Affordability

Going global can be very expensive, which is why smaller companies often start their international venturing within e-marketplaces. These are more than online trade fairs – the intention is that transactions can take place. The benefit for suppliers is that potential new customers from around the world can find them and try them. In the case of establishing new international key accounts, e-marketplaces are where new suppliers can be found by business buyers. Business buyers perceive that e-marketplaces give them access to new sources of supply and the ability to manage all sources of supply more cost-effectively. This does not necessarily mean a focus on driving down prices. E-marketplaces should be a showcase for the value that suppliers can bring. In the UK, the Chartered Institute of Purchasing and Supply has a partnership with Applegate, which focuses on marketplace information and e-commerce services for procurement professionals.

Compared to the costs of hosting stands at trade shows overseas and advertising in a variety of countries, e-marketplaces offer cost-effectiveness to suppliers too. As mentioned earlier, e-marketplaces can lead on to the deployment of contract sales organizations or recruiting key account managers where opportunities emerge that have long-term potential.

> Compared to the costs of hosting stands at trade shows overseas and advertising in a variety of countries, e-marketplaces offer cost-effectiveness to suppliers too.

Balancing activity and control

Ultimately, as with any business expansion, the managers of a company that wants to serve key accounts in several countries or find new key

Figure 8.3 Assessing internationalization risk

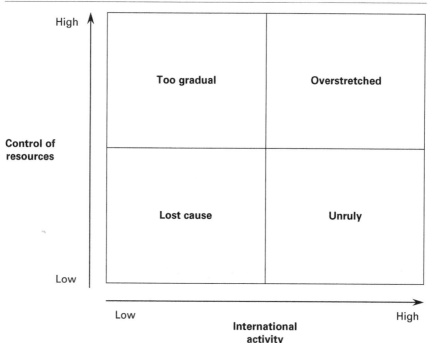

SOURCE adapted from Solberg (2012)

accounts in other countries has to control its expansion without stifling it. Figure 8.3 shows the possibilities and risks. Most companies would aspire to operate somewhere in the middle – controlling resources to a reasonable degree while activities are expanding at a reasonable pace. The options in Figure 8.3 are summarized in Table 8.3.

Table 8.3   Assessing internationalization risk

Too gradual	If internationalization is not undertaken at a sufficient pace, competitors will take up opportunities. This is particularly true in key accounts. The suppliers who are able to serve them in the widest variety of locations are likely to take a dominant share of purse.
Overstretched	High control of high levels of activity may sound ideal, but it introduces different risks. The fixed cost of control, such as local subsidiaries or supply points, may be a burden, especially if a key account wants support in idiosyncratic markets with few other opportunities to spread the customer portfolio in that location.
Lost cause	If there is no momentum for internationalization, a company may as well recognize its constraints and stay local. This will also constrain the type and variety of accounts that it can consider key.
Unruly	Achieving high levels of activity with minimal control probably means that intermediaries such as sales agents, or the key account, are reaping most of the benefit.

SOURCE adapted from Solberg (2012)

Thinking about our case study, IOQ, it seems that all of these risks apply. They must find a way to manage a lot of new international activities in a way that is consistent and will appear achievable and plausible to XYZ.

Global account management capabilities

Once on the global journey with key accounts, the challenge is to keep them. Change is a constant in most business environments, but when operating globally, the potential for sudden change in some market in which you operate is greater. Therefore it is important to make sure that capabilities are developed that are useful in managing business relationships on a global scale.

Assessing possible market change

Market sensing and customer insight is critical. The more that you know, and the more you refresh and re-examine your knowledge, the more likely it is that risks can be managed. Some global companies are very adept at scenario planning the possibilities in a variety of international markets, assessing what their impact might be and compiling contingency plans. An example of a diagram that is often used in scenario planning is shown in Figure 8.4.

How probable is it that X will happen? What impact could it have? When it comes to environmental factors in international markets,

Figure 8.4   Example diagram used in scenario planning

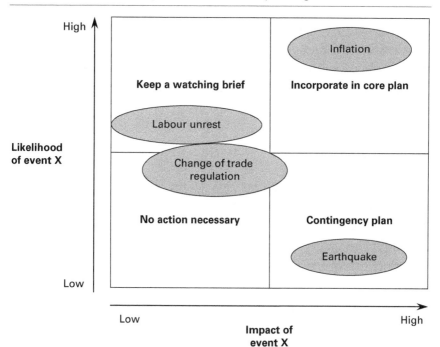

SOURCE adapted from Hillson (2002)
NOTE risks/events can have positive outcomes as well as negative, eg changes in trade regulation may be liberalization, which could create opportunities

these questions are critical. Using this analysis tool should lead to plans being drawn up for the most probable scenarios and contingency plans being drawn up for the highest-impact scenarios.

The same procedure can also apply to customer events and competitor activity. (This leads us back to the analysis underpinning key account plans in general, and the need for scenarios and simulations, discussed in Chapter 5.)

> *To be able to provide integrated and consistent service while recognizing local market sensitivities can be a strong capability to offer.*

Value creation

Many global key accounts ask for global service from suppliers in the expectation of standardization of products, processes, service and prices across international markets. At the same time, the whole purpose of being a key account is to receive a customized solution. The key account itself has to determine a balance between global standardization and closeness to local markets. In fact, to be able to provide integrated and consistent service while recognizing local market sensitivities can be a strong capability to offer, as explained by Simon Derbyshire earlier in this chapter.

Reconfiguration

Earlier on, we mentioned real options theory. We know from recent studies that there is a risk of a KAM organization becoming as bureaucratic as whatever came before it. In international markets, the ability to change channels, supply routes and contract terms in short periods of time is likely to be necessary.

Closing thoughts

In this chapter, we have considered:

- the desirability of going global with key accounts or in pursuit of new key accounts;

- the enablers and inhibitors of international expansion, including cultural awareness;

- control factors and risk.

KAM is increasingly an international and/or global phenomenon, and smaller companies planning to serve larger customers must be prepared to go global with them.

Now, what would happen with IOQ?

First of all, they have to call together all the subsidiaries and partners that they have already, in order to test out all the implications of being a global supplier to a global account. These would include:

- how to achieve process excellence worldwide;

- cross-cultural management;

- anticipating the sheer volume of communications required in global account teams, and with the customer;

- attention to detail in managing the scope of work;

- ensuring that current and future partners 'buy-in' to the offer made to the key account.

What has happened in some situations like this is that like-minded suppliers to a global conglomerate faced with the same challenge find each other and form alliances, which may in time become acquisitions or mergers.

Action list

Consider which of these matrices and checklists you can use to improve your international potential.

Learn more about the languages and cultures in your key account.

References

Baum, M, Schwens, C and Kabst, R (2012) Determinants of different types of born globals, in *Handbook of Research on Born Globals*, ed M Gabrielsson and VH Kirpalani, pp 36–45, Edward Elgar Publishing, Cheltenham

Harich, KR and LaBahn, DW (1998) Enhancing international business relationships: a focus on customer perceptions of salesperson role performance including cultural sensitivity, *Journal of Business Research*, **42** (1), pp 87–101

Hillson, D (2002) Extending the risk process to manage opportunities, *International Journal of Project Management*, **20** (3), pp 235–40

Knight, R (2015) How to run a meeting of people from different cultures, *Harvard Business Review*, 4 December

Murphy, WH and Li, N (2015) Government, company, and dyadic factors affecting key account management performance in China: propositions to provoke research, *Industrial Marketing Management*, **51**, pp 115–21

Solberg, CA (2012) The born global dilemma: trade-off between rapid growth and control, in *Handbook of Research on Born Globals*, ed M Gabrielsson and VH Kirpalani, pp 57–70, Edward Elgar Publishing, Cheltenham

The risks of key account management

09

We start this chapter with a case study based on some real examples of over-reliance on a key account.

CASE STUDY Wireless Devices Inc

Wireless Devices were founded in 1910, making parts for radio sets. They soon established regular business with KZQ Inc, a major electrical goods company. As demand for radio and other forms of home entertainment expanded, KZQ Inc became the market leader in North America and Europe, and Wireless Devices grew alongside their powerful customer. They became a big manufacturing brand too. The relationship was cordial. Joint product development was normal. In fact, KZQ actively discouraged Wireless from diversifying with other customers and into other sectors. They behaved in a similar way with other long-standing suppliers. As the dominant player in the supply chain, they believed that a quasi-vertical marketing system from raw materials through to the end customer was strategically desirable. This was a common approach in the United States and parts of Europe from the 1930s through to the 1970s. It was similar to the Japanese keiretsu *system of supply chain interdependencies, but not so formal.*

Such a system relies on a lot of goodwill. It also relies on relative economic stability. As manufacturing developed in the Far East throughout the 1980s and 1990s, shareholders expected the major corporations they financed to find cheaper sources of parts. Companies like KZQ had to bargain hard with home suppliers or access new suppliers in new markets, even if it was still somewhat risky to source parts on the other side of the world. Or they could do both. Of course, the process had to be fair. There would be a huge relisting exercise for a new generation of technology, and only a few would survive. Wireless Devices were not used to bidding on such a huge scale. So much business had been too regular for so many decades. KZQ was 30 per cent of their turnover. One dreadful day in 2002, they were told that they had not been listed for KZQ's new technology platform. Despite the fact that Wireless had other customers and would still have a few years to run out their existing business with KZQ, the stock market turned on the company, perceiving the failure to be endorsed to supply a new technology platform as an indication of lack of innovation. Wireless Devices crashed.

They had been doing business with KZQ for many decades. There were few formalized contracts, and no specific exit plan. Some suppliers in the same situation were poised to sue KZQ for compensation. Wireless Devices was bought up by a competitor who had been successful in the bid for KZQ's new technology platform.

We have discussed the principles of marketing in B2B sectors and the concept of key account management (KAM). We have examined the purchasing profession's view, how to make meaningful value propositions, how to plan for success in individual key accounts and how to allocate resources to KAM as a capability for the company, including the potential for making your KAM international or global. Many years of best practice and diligent research support KAM as a positive approach to winning and sustaining profitable major customers. However, it is not a panacea for all sales challenges. Your company secretary will have a risk register that is regularly presented to the board of directors for discussion. We should consider some of the things that might appear on it as a result of pursuing key account strategies. These all need to be assessed for the probability that they might occur, and the impact they might have, so that informed decisions can be made about how to manage them (see Figure 9.1).

Figure 9.1 Standard risk management model (adapted from a variety of models)

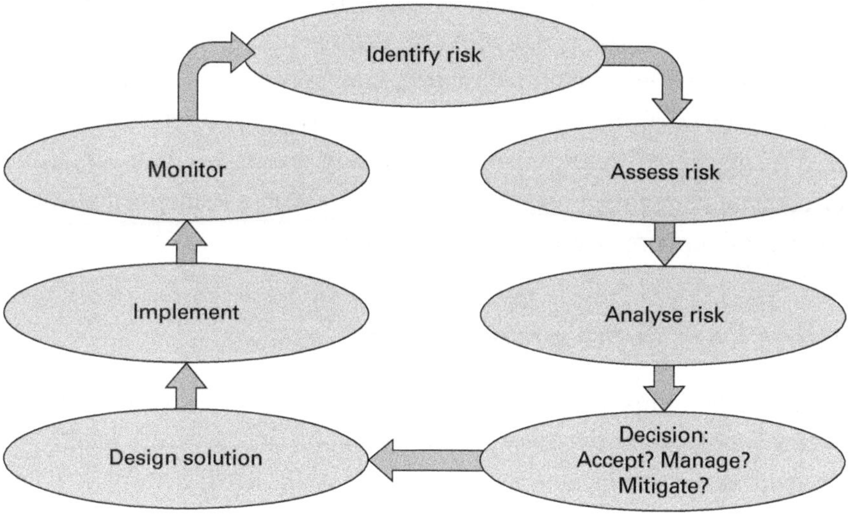

Financial risk

Over-focusing resources on strategic accounts

If one customer represents more than 10 per cent of your turnover, the company secretary is probably very worried. It is not unheard of for customers that have been key accounts for decades to change their supply strategy and leave dependent suppliers in the lurch. A well-known retailer was known for encouraging suppliers to see them as a dominant key account, until they decided there were cheaper sources. A subsequent court case for compensation was not wholly successful, as the suppliers had embraced the risk of working almost exclusively for that retailer. It is fantastic to win and grow business with a key account, but the capabilities generated in that relationship should be transferred into broadening the customer portfolio.

As discussed in Chapter 3, there are a variety of non-key customers, and many of them can be just as profitable. Some of them are tomorrow's key accounts. So, to assure the board, the sales director needs to be managing the complete customer portfolio, generating new business as well as nurturing existing customers, and he or she must ensure that there is an exit plan for any key account representing a significant proportion of turnover. Generally, companies do not want the bad publicity that can be associated with dumping long-term suppliers and destroying jobs. Nevertheless, they will dump suppliers – who have done nothing wrong – when economic circumstances require it, or if their technology is superseded, or if their product simply goes out of fashion.

Using KAM in the wrong places

It is worth noting that in some industrial sectors the culture in the sector is not supportive of a partnership approach. If 'arm's length' or even adversarial supplier–customer relationships are the norm, it is not impossible to overcome it, but a company would have to do so very selectively. The majority of customers might take the extra service and still play suppliers off against one another for price. KAM is a significant long-term investment and has to be deployed where returns are best.

Legal risk

The risks of quasi-partnerships

> It is the customer who is normally most sensitive to avoiding 'lock-in' to particular suppliers, but suppliers should also beware of 'lock-in' to particular customers.

It is the customer who is normally most sensitive to avoiding 'lock-in' to particular suppliers, but suppliers should also beware of 'lock-in' to particular customers. While tightly formed supply chains with cross-ownership have been quite normal in Japan (*keiretsu*), in the United States and most Western European countries it would raise concern with legislators about anti-competitive behaviour. If there is no formal joint venture and companies are co-developing products, sharing processes and co-branding offerings, the company secretary might be reaching for the risk register. Close partnerships are a source of innovation and cost-savings, but any sharing of intellectual property or co-investment needs to be properly arranged.

> While little has been made public in the press or the literature, workshop discussions with executives have uncovered several instances where companies in close collaborations with major customers have been issued a 'yellow card' by regulators. Competition regulators are increasingly taking the view that close collaboration between buyer and seller is potentially anti-competitive.
>
> Piercy and Lane (2006: 24)

'Distortion of trade'

Some companies are becoming very wary of any type of hospitality – and suppliers need to be very sensitive to customers' policies.

It is quite normal for a key account manager to take a customer decision-maker out for a meal when discussions spill over lunch or into the evening. Similarly, combining a seminar about a new product with a sporting event is a widely used opportunity to get time with customers. However, some companies are becoming very wary of any type of hospitality – and suppliers need to be very sensitive to customers' policies, and to the law. In the UK, any distortion of trade could be challenged by a competitor, whether it is discounting, hospitality or gifts. Perceptions of trade being distorted are very contextual. Sponsoring a skittles match for a whole department as a regular annual event might be seen as acceptable, whereas a lavish meal for a particular individual before a contract is about to be signed would be suspicious. The contexts include when the event takes place, who benefits, where it is held, how much is spent and the degree of information balanced with entertainment. Common sense should prevail.

Most purchasing managers are members or fellows of the Chartered Institute of Purchasing and Supply, and will be very clear about the company policy on hospitality for them or any other decision-makers.

Extract from the CIPS code of conduct:

I will enhance and protect the standards of the profession by...
not accepting inducements or gifts (other than any declared gifts of
nominal value that have been sanctioned by my employer);
not allowing offers of hospitality or those with vested interests to influence,
or be perceived to influence, my business decisions.

https://www.cips.org/Documents/About%20CIPS/CIPS_Code_of_
conductv2_10_9_2013.pdf

However, suppliers should also be careful about being too miserly. Most busy executives would not be too pleased if they travelled for hours to a supplier's seminar and were only offered machine coffee and soggy sandwiches as refreshment.

Organizational risk

Failing to underpin KAM with a robust infrastructure

In the early days of KAM, purchasing managers would often complain that while they liked a particular supplier's key account manager and their professional approach, they observed that he or she had responsibility without authority. In order words, the key account manager was the 'Aunt Sally' where they threw their complaints, but did not have the power within the supplier organization to make value happen for the customer. Most companies have now evolved, and have KAM infrastructures where value delivery is directed by the key account manager. However, many companies are still trying to perfect the right structure for KAM, particularly global account management. It is not easy when key account teams include multiple functions, multiple product divisions and multiple country organizations. How can they all agree to deliver the same high standards or service at every touchpoint with the key account? Somehow, they have to do so.

However the organization chart is configured, an underlying principle should be that key account managers must have regular contact with the board so that they are seen to have symbolic power. How many key accounts you have could be a factor of how many key accounts board members can reasonably sponsor. Another guiding principle could be the streamlining of the key account manager's expensive time. If it is eaten up with everyday fire-fighting because of organizational blocks, that indicates a weak infrastructure. The organizational design needs to enable the key account manager to be 'intrapreneurial' (in other words, to facilitate internal change in an entrepreneurial way). Many companies have found ways of accommodating intrapreneurship in product/service development. It is also necessary for customer development.

> *An underlying principle should be that key account managers must have regular contact with the board so that they are seen to have symbolic power.*

Losing the plot

Never forget how difficult it is for key account managers and key account team members to be brand ambassadors for the company to the key account, and advocates of the key account within the company. This 'boundary-spanning' role inevitably causes stress, and senior managers should look out for signs of it. There is a fine line between the positive concept of 'boundary spanning' between supplier and customer to achieve objectives for both, and the negative concept of 'role ambiguity'. Role ambiguity occurs when customer-facing staff are confused about what they are supposed to be achieving for which stakeholder. We know from many decades of research that there is one consistent message from studies of sales productivity – role ambiguity has a negative effect on it.

> The role of the key account team is by its very nature boundary spanning, requiring the team to *'sell'* in two directions – the obvious selling of their employer's services into the key account, and perhaps the less obvious – selling the merits of the key account internally within their own organization. This is one of these fine lines that needs to be carefully navigated within the context of KAM, especially in relation to the

aggressive 'selling' of the key account into their own organization. Being over-zealous in pushing the case of the key account internally can be met with comments such as 'Remember who you work for!', or 'Remember who is paying your salary!' In extreme cases the key account team can be described as having 'defected to the other side', by which it is meant that they have lost perspective and are no longer occupying a boundary role/position. They have effectively become too influenced by, and have fallen too far into the key account's culture and organizational politics; the only solution is to extract and replace them.

In order to prevent this situation occurring, a series of checks and balances need to be put in place by the supplier organization. This can include reducing the onus on a small team by expanding the governance structure, or by having a multi-level governance model. Monthly review meetings with their own senior executives, and regular internal training sessions relating to new offers or services that may be of interest to the key account, all help in keeping the key account team grounded and focused on their primary objective, which is to sell profitable business.

Simon Derbyshire, Vice-President of Capgemini Saudi Arabia
Capgemini: a global leader in consulting, technology and outsourcing services

Loss of skilled staff

Highly skilled key account managers do not grow on trees, and losing them to a competitor, or early retirement, or even to promotion within the company, should be logged as a risk that needs managing. There is a considerable burden on smaller companies when trying to recruit key account managers. Often their brand is not strong enough to secure the people they require. However, we have seen companies use third parties such as interim management agencies and contract sales organizations to deploy key account managers quickly and effectively. Someone does not have to work directly for you to believe in your brand and be an ambassador for it.

Marketing risk

Failing to use KAM to differentiate

We are rather dismayed when sales directors sometimes tell us that the quality of their sales and account management activity is probably not acknowledged by the customer to be superior to their competitors in any particular way. If that is the case after implementing KAM, then something still needs to be done. Of course, competitors may have their own version of KAM. In the IT sector, where most of the major players have highly trained key account managers, how can one company's KAM be different from another? It could be more flexible, more ideas-oriented, better planned, more international or more responsive. KAM is supposed to help companies to beat competitors. As KAM transitioned from best practice to normal practice, the pioneers of KAM have raised their game. KAM has constituent parts – a large variety of assets, processes and skills – and they can differ in combination per company. The quest for the best combination never stops.

Negative critical incidents

When something goes wrong in a key account, it has to be fixed very quickly. We hear of key account managers driving through the night to make sure that they manage the reaction when they deliver an urgently needed part, rather than leaving it to a courier. Filling the key account's shelves with competitors' products when your own delivery has failed is another example. A key account, in return for commitment to a strategic supplier, expects no nasty surprises and a good night's sleep. Even more so, the buying decision-makers expect colleagues to admire them for having chosen such a reliable and easy-to-use supplier. Where there has been strategic bliss at board level between a supplier and key account, but the key account's operations staff feel let down by the supplier, things have ended up in court.

Negative critical incidents (NCIs) are always a risk, but the risk is heightened in key accounts. Even if there is no adverse publicity in the trade press, or legal implications, we have seen in an earlier chapter how purchasing decision-makers take note of the opinion of others when they are assessing a potential supplier. Negative word-of-mouth is as damaging in business sectors as it is on social media for consumer brands.

Ironically, successful recovery from a negative critical incident can convince the customer of your credibility as a supplier, so NCIs are not always a complete disaster. It is accepted that the unexpected happens, especially when innovation is being undertaken. If your contingency plans for failure are more robust than competitors then that could be attractive to customers.

Most organizations use a visual approach to reporting the risk register (as shown in Figure 9.2) – usually red/amber/green (rather than the shades of grey we show here).

Figure 9.2   Risk register

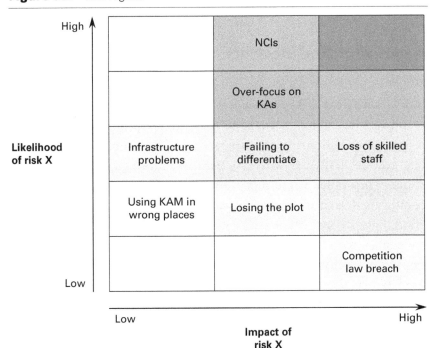

SOURCE adapted from Hillson (2002)

Could KAM go out of fashion?

Some business commentators speculate about a post-KAM world driven by the internet of things and customer analytics engines. Technology does exist to monitor everything that is happening in a customer's machine or in their retail outlet, which can be fed into other information systems to generate a value proposition on the right decision-maker's screen at the right time. Of course, companies should invest in getting the best out of technology wherever they can deploy it cost-effectively, and where the customer finds it helpful rather than frustrating or intrusive.

We hear purchasing managers saying 'please automate non-critical and routine transactions'. We know that many of them have little time to spend discussing 'life, the universe and everything' with suppliers. Nevertheless, when suppliers do have 'thought leadership' to offer in their category, they may win the right to present it. We perceive that KAM has moved on from focusing on the importance of long-term relationships in the 1980s to a focus on evidenced value combined with expectations of innovation. We have always argued that KAM only exists when the supplier understands the customer's needs in depth and can offer specific value that is better than the competitor's offering. It is fairly simple, but many companies still find it difficult to find or develop account managers who can have conversations with senior decision-makers in customers about the financial value-in-use of the solutions they can offer. We admire SKF, who have put so many thousands of examples of the value-in-use of their products on their website (http://www.skf.com/uk/knowledge-centre/index.html).

In 2011, the concept of the 'challenger' sale was launched (Dixon and Adamson, 2011). Several observers of the media hype around the book came away with two ideas. First, that relationship sellers were not successful; and second, that the only salespeople who were successful were telling the customer that they were wrong (ie making a challenge). This was unfair to the book, which explains in depth the nuances within the research. We perceive that the concept of the challenger sale was reinforcing the body of knowledge that tells us that key account managers should become trusted advisers and therefore be able to have difficult conversations with customers about how they might be doing things better. They do not earn that right without being good relationship builders. Obviously, relationship building without discussing fundamentally strategic issues with the customer's use of your products would be fairly meaningless.

> *There is an enduring and growing demand for people who understand best practice in KAM and who can imagine even better practice and implement it.*

So, we see no immediate signs of the demise of KAM. Arguably, even when people were selling stone tools in return for beads, some customers were perceived to be more important than others. Even if all buying and selling could be designed into artificial intelligence, the fundamentals of KAM would have to be part of the programme. If anything, the increasing interest in professional institutes for consultative selling, and the increasing availability of sales and account management qualifications in higher-education institutions, demonstrates that there is an enduring and growing demand for people who understand best practice in KAM and who can imagine even better practice and implement it.

Despite the risks we have discussed here, and more that might be applicable in particular scenarios, we do see a future for KAM, and this is the topic of our final chapter.

References

Dixon, M and Adamson, B (2011) *The Challenger Sale: Taking control of the customer conversation*, Penguin, New York

Hillson, D (2002) Extending the risk process to manage opportunities, *International Journal of Project Management*, 20 (3), pp 235–40

Piercy, NF and Lane, N (2006) The hidden risks in strategic account management strategy, *Journal of Business Strategy*, 27 (1), pp 18–26

The future of key account management

10

We would like to thank our colleagues Dr Rodrigo Guesalaga, Ralph Baillie, Dr Sue Holt, Kate Davies and Dr Ian Speakman whose report 'The future of key account management' has provided inspiration for this chapter. We also draw your attention to the appendix to this chapter, which reports on our past predictions for key account management (KAM).

> With the world economy in a significant state of flux, the only certainty is that things are not going to be dull in the coming period. The continued push in establishing international trade deals and opening up new markets will become more significant. For this to be successful, more effort and focus will be needed in addressing differences in national culture and adapting KAM and ABM approaches appropriately.
>
> Simon Derbyshire, Vice-President of Capgemini Saudi Arabia
> *Capgemini, a global leader in consulting, technology and outsourcing services*

The business environment has suffered several shocks in the past few years, and ways of doing business have to change. Sometimes it is a matter of continuous improvement and sometimes ways of doing business have to be rapidly reconfigured. It is easy to say that the best business-growth strategy involves applying the right resources to the right opportunities, but we also need the capabilities and processes to fix those connections together. Of course, it has to be fixed with a 'post-it note'-type glue so that the company does not get locked in to practices that outlive their usefulness.

The discussions about the future of KAM fall into several categories. By far the questions that are most often raised are about the way KAM is organized. Many companies have tried unique KAM divisions and various forms of hard and soft matrix management. The last thing we want is KAM to be a rigid bureaucratic hierarchy slapped on top of other company hierarchies such as product divisions or geographic divisions. Discussions about the definition and redefinition of key accounts are also popular. This is partly linked to technological development such as account-based marketing (ABM), but also the internet of things, which can add exciting new possibilities to automated personalization. Changes in buyer behaviour and the constant challenge to co-create value are also hot topics. We have positioned this category last because it is perhaps where most uncertainty lies. If customers were to decide that there is no value in KAM, it would die. We are encouraged by life-cycle research, which suggests that while some customers' interest in KAM could wane, others would emerge who need strategic suppliers. We note that the principles of accountability, traceability and sustainability in supply chains are increasingly occupying senior managers' discussions.

Organizing for KAM

Strategic accounts served by 'dedicated' members are relatively scarce because few customers require a high level of dedicated resources. At the same time, the most common manner in which firms serve strategic accounts is by utilizing 'fluid' teams, which tend to have dynamic membership rather than dedicated members.

Bradford *et al* (2012)

It is fair to say that, for most companies, the number of key accounts that require dedicated teams are few, but where they are needed they can be substantial. In global suppliers serving global customers, perhaps with many partner organizations, we have seen key account teams of over 200 people. Those team members need to maintain consistent levels of service to the customer across different physical environments, time zones and cultures, which is quite a leadership challenge for the key account manager.

So, should there be a Key Accounts Division, or should there be some kind of matrix structure? Having a key account division runs the risk of creating a competing bureaucracy and power structure, and having a matrix can create conflict and confusion, even though it is designed to resolve it. We talked in Chapter 7 about the challenges of giving mixed messages to employees trying to do their best for their functional line manager, their regional manager and the key account manager. The board has to provide a framework of understanding and prioritization. Where there is conflict between competing interests (which will not always be the case) what comes first? Many companies have decided – customer first, functional or product interest second and country third. But of course, it is exceptions that prove the rule. If the customer makes a demand that is going to bankrupt the company, no account manager will agree to it, and rightly so. A spirit of creative conflict is required if the key account team is going to have innovative ideas. Anyone who takes on any role involving account management has to be able to cope with some ambiguity in their working life. The business environment is constantly changing; customers change within it and need their suppliers to be change agents too.

One thing we observe that has a significant impact on the financial performance of key accounts is that the involvement of senior managers is critical. We have already discussed this in Chapter 7. But it is worth repeating as it is unlikely to change in the future. Assumptions are made about the need for each key account to have a senior manager as a sponsor, or at least companies need a sub-committee of the board to oversee key accounts. Christoph Senn's (2006) case study suggested that this is a vital factor in rapidly growing account share in key accounts:

> Companies that commit to creating such an executive engagement process can expect to benefit from hard-to-copy intimacy with their customers, which in turn results in new, sustainable sources of competitive advantage.
>
> Senn (2006: 27)

The question then arises – how many key accounts can any board member manage? Probably, not very many – if the sponsorship is to be of meaningful depth. We should note that it takes a certain type of executive sponsorship to be productive:

> KAM is more likely to flourish under an enquiring type of leader (eg who asks 'what's the problem, how do we know that, what can we do?'), rather than one who dictates a solution based on past experience.
>
> Guesalaga *et al* (2016: 15)

So, when considering how many really key accounts we have, perhaps the answer is – how many can the board sponsor? If the board ever loses interest in KAM, or feels overwhelmed or bored by it, the internecine problems between departments delivering services to key accounts could re-emerge. That would increase costs to serve and increase the risk of competitors spotting an opportunity to make a move on your key accounts.

In the Cranfield report (Guesalaga *et al*, 2016), practitioners have also mentioned a number of questions for the future, which we have discussed in previous chapters. The constant demand for key account managers to balance fighting today's fire with strategizing for the future, balance short-term financial target with long-term relational goals, be the standard bearer for the supplier to the customer and be the standard bearer for the customer to colleagues, to have credibility from the factory floor to the boardroom in both organizations, to be an 'intrapreneur' and change agent within the customer and their own employer... these challenges do not go away. They are why the key account manager needs to have senior status, sophisticated skills and a sophisticated measurement and rewards package. We rest our case. We have also mentioned the increasing need for all members of the key account team to perceive themselves as part of a selling team, and the trend for key account teams to extend beyond company boundaries into supply chains and networks. We expect this to be more accentuated over time.

Defining key accounts

Chapter 3 discusses in detail how key accounts can be defined and selected. Research strongly suggests that it is errors in selection that are the first sign of failure in KAM programmes. As mentioned below, the challenge to select and reselect very effectively is only likely to increase in the future.

The evolution of KAM is also likely to involve increasing levels of focus and specificity involving much deeper qualification of a customer and their ability to satisfy pre-qualified account attractiveness criteria. This is just a reflection of the fact that KAM requires an investment for it to be effective and successful in delivering the required returns. The levels of investment available are increasingly finite, as is the capacity for developing deep relationships in meaningful contexts between executives. This targeting of fire power, in the context of KAM, probably falls under the definition of account-based marketing.

Simon Derbyshire, Vice-President of Capgemini Saudi Arabia
Capgemini, a global leader in consulting,
technology and outsourcing services

Changing technology

Among our practitioner contributors, the role of technology was definitely a 'hot topic'. We are very grateful to Karen Bell for the discussion below about how technology is affecting KAM in the pharmaceutical sector:

The future of KAM

As the pharmaceutical industry becomes more patient- and outcomes-focused in order to gain government/insurance company acceptance of its medicines, companies now need to consider how they keep the patient in mind at every step. They are increasingly required to clearly demonstrate how their medicines benefit the patient. Today's key account managers need to understand the buying organizations' needs and indeed the local health economy agendas in more detail than ever before. They should be able to articulate a strong value proposition to an increasingly diverse range of stakeholders. If they fail to do this, they run the risk of alienating these important customers, and diminishing the value that pharmaceutical companies can add.

The future will see the most successful companies increasingly employing individuals who are both competent and comfortable engaging with payers, providers and clinicians on a range of topics, and that can transition between market access, promotional and service development activities. Recruiting, developing and retaining these key individuals should be a critical part of a company's sales strategy.

Around half of today's healthcare professionals rely heavily on digital and remote channels as a primary source for medical enquiries and medical education, so it is essential that companies and their key account managers evolve their approach to customer interactions. Key account managers of the future will be required to possess or develop information technology and digital capability, as well as remote customer service skills. It has always been essential to effectively influence administrative or support staff over the phone in order to gain access to the healthcare professional. It is now equally and increasingly important that key account managers engage effectively with healthcare professionals over the phone and on remote detailing platforms, especially those healthcare professionals who are less familiar with remote media. Familiarity with remote (telephone) promotional detailing, use of digital platforms such as WebEx, and the remote coaching of healthcare professionals to engage with these new delivery channels are key skills that all key account managers will require in the near future.

It is likely that the future will also see the continued emergence of 'hybrid' key account managers. The hybrid or multichannel sales approach is where there is a mixture of face-to-face and remote detailing, typically with around one to two days per week spent on the remote calls, with activities/remote days often flexed around the availability of customers rather than having set days for each type of call. Hybrid key account managers can also supplement their remote detailing activity with other remote contact methods, including e-mailing of approved promotional materials and signposting healthcare professionals to medical education or patient support resources, although it is essential that the appropriate permissions have been gained from the healthcare professional before doing so.

Hybrid key account managers will become increasingly common in the future, but they will only be successful if companies develop and implement a robust strategy for this approach, giving careful consideration to the type of individuals who are suitable for this role, and ongoing training development. The right technology, systems and governance are also required in order that all customer interactions are delivered in a code-compliant way. Ideally, all remote interactions with customers should be recorded and regularly monitored, which can be an onerous undertaking for many companies.

Successful co-existence of face-to-face calling and remote detailing, or the combination 'hybrid key account manager' approach is dependent on selecting the preferred delivery method for that customer. Pharma companies need to be able to effectively map preference and deliver calls via the selected channel using a variety of digital tools and content, as well as employing adequately skilled representatives. In addition, they need the supporting technology, systems and processes to ensure all calls are delivered in a professional and compliant way so that they do not fall foul of industry Code of Practice rules that apply to remote detailing.

Most importantly, companies need to recruit, train and develop individuals who are easily able to plan and deliver a multichannel approach to their interactions with customers, as well as being confident and proficient with both technology and the delivery of sales calls through the remote channels of the phone and internet.

Karen Bell, Business Development Director at Ashfield,
part of UDG Healthcare plc
Ashfield, part of UDG Healthcare plc, is a global leader in commercialization services for the pharmaceutical and healthcare industry, operating across two broad areas of activity: commercial and clinical services, and communications services. It focuses on supporting healthcare professionals and patients at all stages of the product life cycle.
The division provides field and contact-centre sales teams, healthcare communications, patient support, audit, advisory, medical information and event management services to over 300 healthcare companies in over 50 countries. For more information please go to: www.ashfieldhealthcare.com

Technology-driven ABM

Although we have included a chapter on ABM, it is worth reflecting again on the growing interdependence between KAM and account-based marketing. The relationship between marketing and account management needs strategic management attention.

The future of KAM relies on a more knowledge-driven approach to selling, which will impact every stage of the process: from identifying the needs, to demonstrating value, to closing the deals. Marketing practitioners have always sought to leverage data to better engage their audience, while KAM has built its knowledge through personal relationships. ABM brings together the best of both worlds.

First, ABM will enable marketing and sales management to collaborate on common frameworks to identify and categorize key accounts in a more pragmatic fashion. It will help profiling and analysing complex buying processes, whose patterns and influences are unique to each customer organization. As a result, more effective strategies will be developed to optimize customer engagement and to allocate resources.

Key account managers will need to step outside their comfort zone by selling beyond their traditional contacts. This means finding new needs across different lines of business. ABM will provide data to support this. It will capture buying signals from digital channels in order to identify more accurately potential opportunities that will contribute to the overall key account strategy.

Finally, ABM will empower key account managers to differentiate their value proposition and build credibility by telling a story that is truly relevant to each customer. In the digital era, buyers are more knowledgeable than ever, and they would favour peer recommendations or social media over a sales pitch. For key account managers, being able to talk about their singular challenges and context will increasingly be the key to success.

Cédric Belliard, Field Marketing Manager
for a global technology company

The Strategic Account Management Association, which represents a large number of global companies employing key account managers, has focused recently on the effect of digitalization:

The future of strategic, key and global account management is perhaps the one topic pressing on the minds of practitioners and experts working in this field that creates feelings of excitement, uncertainty and apprehension, all at the same time. The reason is the accelerating change occurring as a result of the exponential growth of digital technologies. In January 2017, the Strategic Account Management Association (SAMA) and research partner Kaj Storbacka, Professor of Markets and Strategy at the University of Auckland Business School, published its initial assessment of the impact of digital technologies on strategic account management in *The Digitalization Drive: Elevating strategic account management.* Perhaps the most important insight gained through this first phase of research was 'the realization that changes in SAM practices are driven not only by the emergence of new digital technologies but, even more importantly, by the modifications in strategy and business models that digitalization drives. Consequently, SAM programmes need to be elevated into an even more strategic role: driving the digitally enabled strategic transformation of both firms and customers.'

As one SAMA member remarked in an earlier 2016 SAMA research study, 'Changes and Predictions Affecting Strategic Account Management', digital technologies are 'changing the rules of the game' and affecting the core nature of strategic customer–supplier relationships. Customers now interact through the internet and, in 'omnichannel' style, acquire information and insight on suppliers, products, services and alternative sourcing where they can chat, choose, comment and collect immense amounts of data, all before talking with a specific supplier.

The implications of digitalization force SAM programmes to redefine themselves on multiple dimensions. The over-arching change trajectory is that *SAM is becoming more strategic*, finally truly acknowledging its label. Among the many new avenues of opportunity that digital technologies present to KAM/SAM organizations are:

- The use of advanced analytics – where the real value of analytics relates to creating more valuable products and services.

- Automation technologies – using smart machines, autonomous agents, algorithmic applications; a major application being ABM, which considers and communicates with each prospective or active customer as a market of one, instead of spreading marketing resources based on segments or markets. ABM tailors an approach for each account with the aim to support the customer journey in achieving its goals. Tools and technologies such as CRM, marketing automation and advanced analytics make ABM much more scalable.

- A shift from exchange value to use value – where use-value thinking assumes that the central value creation in a market happens when a customer uses a good or service. For KAM/SAM this implies a need to become even more embedded into the strategic account process of value creation and to harness all data that can be used for this purpose.

- An expansion of the customer–supplier ecosystem – where SAM, as a boundary-crossing activity, needs to expand its view from customer relationships to more complex set-ups of collaborating organizations.

- Application programming interfaces (APIs). An API is a set of routines, protocols and tools for building software applications – essentially a description of the way that one piece of software asks another program to perform a service. What APIs make possible is a dramatic increase in collaboration between organizations and the widespread availability of APIs has made the modern internet experience possible. More importantly, APIs are allowing many firms to grow business and innovate at extraordinary rates by sharing services with external firms.

Regarding their role and responsibilities, key, strategic and global account managers need to think of themselves less as consultative account managers and more as community facilitators. By being present on social media and other platforms they can regularly connect to customers and get educated on new opportunities for value creation. Firms need to provide individuals involved in KAM/SAM (and their teams) opportunities to develop their digital acumen, in the same way as they have helped them earlier to develop their financial acumen related to value-based sales.

Digitalization depreciates the value of experience and changes the nature of expertise. The outcome is that business decisions will be based less on experience (as there often cannot be any experience in this new age) and more on what the data and the related analytics tell us. Perhaps most critically, the SAM's role and the SAM process need to be designed in such a way that it enables distributed leadership in a collaborative process; and, SAM programmes need to embrace the opportunities that digital technologies make possible in terms of efficiency and effectiveness.

Bernard Quancard, President and CEO, Strategic Account Management Association (SAMA)

SAMA is a unique non-profit association with more than 10,000 members worldwide. SAMA focuses solely on helping establish strategic, key and global account management as a separate profession, career path and proven corporate strategy for growth. For more information, go to www.strategicaccounts.org

S   A   M   A

The use of social media

Despite its popular reputation for hosting trivia, some social media platforms are suitable for business activity. Most decision-makers are comfortable seeking contacts and exchanging business messages via LinkedIn. This suggests that social media is more applicable to new business development than mature B2B relationships (see Table 10.1), but as can be seen from the quote from Simon Derbyshire, overleaf, key account managers are already using social media to improve their results, and it is likely that social media will become an embedded method of market scanning and communication for new generations of key account managers.

Table 10.1   Social media use

Communication Purpose	Use of Social Media by Key Account Managers
Identity	Having a presence that clarifies professional identity
Credibility	Present values and expertise, via membership of groups, sharing posts, creating a blog
Connection	Reaching out to decision-makers in key accounts, perhaps by introductions from first connections
Retention	Using social media as a research resource, to understand what customers are doing and what competitors are doing
Engagement	Even when relationships have shifted to face-to-face meetings, connections on social media should still be maintained. Checking when contacts change role in customers is important

SOURCE adapted from Lacoste (2016)

The future of KAM, as with the future of many business activities, will involve information, digital and social media technology. An Aberdeen Group study back in 2012 showed that 64 per cent of sales teams using social selling met their key performance indicators (KPIs), as compared to 49 per cent of sales teams that did not use social media in their sales processes. Sales teams using social selling also had better customer renewal rates and sales forecast accuracy. Whilst this is not KAM, it will become part of the future for KAM teams and organizations, including their customers.

The industrial gathering and use of social media data is already happening, and being used to understand perceptions and sentiment, which in turn is influencing brand, marketing, PR and promotional strategies.

Whilst social media is not in heavy use today by key account managers, I would argue that this is a generational issue. In both the key account and the supplier organizations there are a generation of people who started work prior to the age of computers, and for whom social media is not a natural way to engage with someone. As the members of generation Y become more senior and occupy senior KAM and customers' roles, social and digital media usage will be a de facto norm. This phenomenon will experience considerable acceleration when generation Z takes to the helm, for whom a world without digital and social media is completely incomprehensible, and in which building relationships using these technologies is completely natural and to be expected.

Simon Derbyshire, Vice-President of Capgemini Saudi Arabia

Capgemini, a global leader in consulting, technology and outsourcing services

An ongoing debate – what is value and how is it shared?

Do we really understand co-creation of value?

For many centuries, concepts of value were easy. Someone took some raw materials, added some value through their own skill and sold a product to someone else who consumed it. This led to product-driven companies. In technology-driven sectors, if huge corporations became remote from customers and failed to invent what they wanted, new companies would come along and do it and those companies would become the new market leaders. In the past 20 years, customers have become more interested in 'value-in-use' of products and more inclined to engage with suppliers in discussions about what products or services they want. Consumers can be consulted over the internet about new ranges and service concepts, and thousands will participate.

Modern views of value are very complex. The creators of an extremely influential model of value creation, which is association with ideas of 'co-creation', have recently extended their theory to these five principles:

1 Service is the true basis of exchange between suppliers and customers. This does not mean that people do not buy products, but they buy them for what they do rather than what they are.

2 Value is co-created by many people, always including the people who benefit from it. In other words, customers contribute their own skills to gaining value from the solution they are buying. This is why negotiations include consideration for how much service the supplier provides to make something happen in the customer's business versus how much operational risk the customer absorbs.

3 All individuals who are involved in the use of a solution, including the supply network, are part of it. This is why key account teams need to be cross-functional, and collaborating with cross-functional teams in the customer.

4 It is the person who benefits from the value of a solution who determines the degree of its value. Ultimately, it is a perception of value-in-use that is uniquely theirs, and may be very different from another stakeholder's view.

5 Value co-creation is co-ordinated through organizations, their employees and their processes.

Adapted from Vargo and Lusch (2016)

It has been understood for a long time that it is when supplier and customer are investing together that we really know that KAM is working. Some B2B value creation is extremely complex, and may have a very long lifespan – such as the construction of a power plant. In such a case, the co-creation of value is not over until the plant is decommissioned, deconstructed and the land reclaimed. In the case of our Tasty Pies example from Chapter 5, a co-creation of value outlook would certainly encompass joint marketing with the retailer and open discussions about saving costs on cold storage, but it could also involve the nutritional value to the end consumer, the value of meat production to particular farming communities and the ease with which the packaging can be recycled.

Although it has always been the case that value is a matter of perceptions of benefits less the costs you have to get them, there are more ways in which value can be created and consumed, and key account managers will need to continue to develop their skills to understand it.

How conflict, power and dependence erode value

There has been a recent increase in academic studies of what is called the 'dark side' of close business relationships. The difficulties of managing business relationships have never been under-estimated by those involved. We rarely visit a company without hearing an example of decision-makers in an important customer displaying almost psychopathic behaviour in communications and expectations. And of course, the business press offers regular examples of big companies in the supply chain exploiting smaller suppliers. It is inevitable that in any arrangement involving two or more parties, there will be difficulties in adapting to each other's ways of doing business. Normally there is adaptation and communication to ensure that the long-term benefits of the relationship get back on track. Key account managers are usually good at diffusing conflict.

> Business relationships are not inherently good or bad but rather, relationships can produce both simultaneous bright and dark-side effects. Such dark-side effects in their early appearance may be useful if businesses are capable of effective learning. However, failure to learn and adapt within business relationships can allow for early conflict to appear.
> Abosag, Yen and Barnes (2016: 7)

Nevertheless, there is a tendency for business relationships to deteriorate over time. During the growth phase, when things are moving fast, there are incentives for suppliers and customers to make things work. The maturing of business relationships is usually a time for going back out to do some market testing and making new demands on an incumbent supplier in order to justify their status. The contrast between conflict that is normal and tolerable versus the intolerable and unmanageable is shown in Figure 10.1.

The ease of market testing in these days of extensive supplier information, available at the touch of a button, means that suppliers need to be vigilant. Wherever there is potential for conflict and/ or an obvious power imbalance or dependence, there must be robust risk management. Customers also need to beware of abusing their

Figure 10.1   Contrast between forms of conflict

	Tolerable 'Dark-Side'			Intolerable 'Dark-Side'	
Relational issue	Need for learning	Routine problems	Tension due to perceptions of 'slacking'	Communication breakdown	Opportunistic behaviour
Response	Both supplier and customer communicate and adapt		Distancing of key players from relationship	Adversarial negotiations and threats	Potential for exit and court proceedings

SOURCE adapted from Abosag, Yen and Barnes (2016)

power. Suppliers can and do find ways to reconfigure the supply chain network, and there is reputational risk in being perceived as a customer that drives an excessively hard bargain. Hence why some attractive brands will not do business with some retail chains, and why some organizations get disappointing responses to their invitations to tender.

KAM in different cultures

We have devoted a chapter to the internationalization of KAM. We note that public opinion in the United States and Europe now indicates profound disillusionment with globalization. This may lead to companies needing a local presence in more countries, and a greater need for local employment and appreciation of local culture.

Sustainability and values

Early on in this book, we saw how particular organizations, despite being price-sensitive, wanted to make sure that their suppliers shared common values and were willing to support the communities in which they operated. While we have focused on the need for KAM to justify itself in terms of its contribution to a firm's financial success, it is a way of selling that should generate reputational advantage. That advantage can be enhanced by other brand values. We know that sustainability means something to organizations that buy from other organizations, because the Chartered Institute of Purchasing and Supply has a sustainability index:

Developed by procurement experts, CSI (CIPS Sustainability Index) offers a comprehensive, simple, fast and cost-effective online assessment of environmental, economic and social sustainability... it is the only independent, verified measurement tool available, allowing suppliers to prove their sustainability credentials and buyers to obtain essential sustainability information in a more efficient way than via individual and lengthy questionnaires.

As a buyer, CSI gives you a better view of your supply chain and reduces your supplier risk.

As a supplier, CSI helps you to demonstrate excellence in sustainability to industry-approved levels, strengthening information sharing with your customers and supporting your new business bids.

https://www.cips.org/en/cips-for-business/supply-assurance/cips-sustainability-index/

We should note the terminology relating to this index – suppliers who can defend their 'environmental, economic and social sustainability' – ie planet, profit and people – offer a means for CIPS members to reduce supplier risk. There is nothing new in the terminology. The 'triple bottom line' is attributed to the work of John Elkington in the 1990s (see Elkington (1998)), but it is relatively new for this approach to company reporting to play an important role in buying decisions. Key account managers will need more than financial acumen to explain all three elements of this newly popular paradigm.

This return to the concept of value concludes our exploration of the future of key account management. KAM will continue, mainly because customers like it, but it will have to adapt and evolve, like any business strategy. Hopefully, using this concise book, you will be able to keep your KAM programme ahead of business trends.

And finally...

We hope that you have enjoyed this book and know something more about KAM than you did beforehand. We welcome feedback via the publisher or social media or reviews on websites. We wish you good luck in your career.

References

Abosag, I, Yen, DA and Barnes, BR (2016) What is dark about the dark-side of business relationships? *Industrial Marketing Management*, 55, pp 5–9

Bradford, KD, Challagalla, GN, Hunter, GK and Moncrief III, WC (2012) Strategic account management: conceptualizing, integrating, and extending the domain from fluid to dedicated accounts, *Journal of Personal Selling & Sales Management*, 32 (1), pp 41–56

Elkington, J (1998) Partnerships from cannibals with forks: the triple bottom line of 21st-century business, *Environmental Quality Management*, 8 (1), pp 37–51

Guesalaga, R, Baillie, R, Holt, S, Davies, K and Speakman, I (2016) *The Future of Key Account Management*, Cranfield School of Management, Bedford

Lacoste, S (2016) Perspectives on social media and its use by key account managers, *Industrial Marketing Management*, 54, pp 33–43

Senn, C (2006) The executive growth factor: how Siemens invigorated its customer relationships, *Journal of Business Strategy*, 27 (1), pp 27–34

Vargo, SL and Lusch, RF (2016) Institutions and axioms: an extension and update of service-dominant logic, *Journal of the Academy of Marketing Science*, 44 (1), pp 5–23

Appendix 10.1

Nineteen years ago, in our book *Key Account Management: Learning from supplier and customer perspectives*, we made a number of predictions about the future of KAM. In Table 10.2, we reflect on the degree to which we have observed their fruition.

Table 10.2 Reflections on our 1998 predictions for the future of KAM

1998 Prediction	Degree of Success
Value 'cakes' rather than value chains, ie recipes that mix value from different sources	Supply networks are much more complex recipes than they used to be. In particular, we note how key account management does not always relate to immediate links in transactional chains, but to other players in the supply network. Smaller suppliers often have to team with other firms to serve key accounts.
A professional association for account management	In fairness, the Strategic Account Management Association was founded in 1964. However, it was focused on the United States, and it is now a global organization with a much more extensive membership and offerings for members. National Occupational Standards for Sales were established in the UK in 2005, with one of the authors (Beth Rogers) chairing the steering group that delivered them. We note also the development of diplomas in strategic sales and key account management from SAMA, the Chartered Institute of Marketing and the Institute of Sales Management. Recently, the Association for Professional Sales has been founded in the UK, which has made an immediate and positive contribution to creating professional standards and qualifications. The Association of Key Account Management (AKAM) has also been established in Europe.
More focus on key account management in firms	Key accounts have, if anything, become more powerful, and therefore occupy more strategic attention. We have noted in this book that other categories of customer also need strategic resource. However, the complexity of KAM means that it must have board support and attention.
KAM as a means of differentiation	Purchasing decision-makers still report that there are suppliers who are better at KAM than others. The bar keeps rising, and KAM practitioners need to keep investing in their knowledge and skills.
The ethical supply chain – quality, traceability	Scandals in supply chains, such as the horsemeat scandal in the UK in 2013, have ensured that brands are more accountable for their whole supply network than ever before. The concept of the triple bottom line is gaining popularity, and purchasing professionals are likely to expect suppliers to compete on sustainability as an element of value.

(Continued)

Table 10.2 *(Continued)*

1998 Prediction	Degree of Success
Globalization of supplier–customer relationships	This trend has continued, but may be about to go into reverse as many voters in democracies are disillusioned with it, perceiving that it exports their jobs. This may shift the global/local balance in major firms towards local manufacturing and local sourcing.
Consumer sophistication	The availability of information on the internet means that consumers are much more likely to exercise individual and collective buying power, and will lobby brands on issues that matter to them. In business sectors, purchasing continues to shift more resource to information gathering and tries to reduce time spent with suppliers.
Information-technology automating processes	It was an easy prediction. We now embrace the internet of things, which will make processes even more controlled by gadgets themselves without human intervention. This could be a great thing for suppliers who (with customers' permission) embed sensors into products and use the data gathered to help customers use the products more efficiently, and to offer more services based on customer usage patterns.
Smart purchasing	The purchasing profession has indeed extended its influence and skills. It has also automated a great deal of commodity purchasing, enabling more time to focus on strategy.

APPENDIX 1
The McDonald and Rogers 10 guidelines for profitable key account management

There is a lot to digest in this book. But if you can keep these 10 things in mind for key account management (KAM), you should improve results:

1 Understand that KAM is not just super-selling or sales management.

2 Select (and be prepared to reselect) a limited number of key accounts.

3 Categorize key accounts according to their potential for helping you to grow profitably over the planning period.

4 Understand *in depth* the needs of the selected key accounts as organizations and all the professional needs of stakeholders in those key accounts. What are they trying to achieve in their markets and how do your capabilities fit in with that?

5 Categorize the key accounts according to your relative strengths in each, *compared with your major competitors*.

6 Understand your full customer portfolio and use it to balance risks inherent in key accounts.

7 Set realistic objectives and strategies to grow your sales and profits in all customer segments (calculate whether the aggregate key account objectives and strategies create shareholder value).

8 Apply technology to generate insight about key accounts and provide automated services to them.

9 Develop strategic plans for selected key accounts and test them for robustness using simulations that anticipate competitor responses.

10 Ensure that you have highly skilled people as key account managers and give them the necessary authority, support via a key account team and a sensibly balanced short-term and long-term reward package.

Adapted from D Woodburn and M McDonald (2012)
Key Account Management: The definitive guide,
John Wiley & Sons, Chichester

APPENDIX 2
A quiz for key account managers

Senior managers may use this in review meetings with key account managers, and key account managers can use it to prepare for meetings with senior managers.

How well do you know your key account?

Do you know (score out of 10):

1 Your company's proportion of your key account's total spend in your product/service category?

2 Your key account's financial health (return on capital employed, liquidity ratios etc)?

3 Details of your key account's strategic plan?

4 Your key account's business processes (logistics, purchasing, manufacturing, etc)?

5 Your key account's customers/segments/products?

6 Which of your competitors your key account uses, and why and how they rate them?

7 What your key account values from suppliers?

8 The costs to serve your key account?

9 Your key account's projected lifetime value?

10 The risk of losing your key account, and the risks of keeping it?

Adapted from D Woodburn and M McDonald (2012)
Key Account Management: The definitive guide,
John Wiley & Sons, Chichester

APPENDIX 3
Important research articles on key account management

For the curious who would like more detail about the research evidence for key account management (KAM), here is a list of accessible academic articles. Many of these are now free to view via Google Scholar or ResearchGate. Otherwise, access will involve a small fee to the journal publisher.

Abratt, R and Kelly, PM (2002) Customer–supplier partnerships: perceptions of a successful key account management program, *Industrial Marketing Management*, 31 (5), pp 467–76

Al-Husan, FB and Brennan, R (2009) Strategic account management in an emerging economy, *Journal of Business & Industrial Marketing*, 24 (8), pp 611–20

Atanasova, Y and Senn, C (2011) Global customer team design: dimensions, determinants, & performance outcomes, *Industrial Marketing Management*, 40 (2), pp 278–89

Birkinshaw, J, Toulan, O and Arnold, D (2001) Global account management in multinational corporations: theory and evidence, *Journal of International Business Studies*, 32 (2), pp 231–48

Blythe, J (2002) Using trade fairs in key account management, *Industrial Marketing Management*, 31 (7), pp 627–35

Bradford, DK, Challagalla, NG, Hunter, CW and Moncrief, CW (2012) Strategic account management: conceptualizing, integrating, and extending the domain from fluid to dedicated accounts, *Journal of Personal Selling & Sales Management*, 32 (1), pp 41–56

Brehmer, PO and Rehme, J (2009) Proactive and reactive: drivers for key account management programmes, *European Journal of Marketing*, 43 (7/8), pp 961–84

Capon, N and Senn, C (2010) Global customer management programs: how to make them really work, *California Management Review*, 52 (2), pp 32–55

Davies, IA and Ryals, LJ (2009) A stage model for transitioning to KAM, *Journal of Marketing Management*, **25** (9–10), pp 1027–48

Davies, IA and Ryals, LJ (2014) The effectiveness of key account management practices, *Industrial Marketing Management*, **43** (7), pp 1182–94

Friend, SB and Johnson, JS (2014) Key account relationships: an exploratory inquiry of customer-based evaluations, *Industrial Marketing Management*, **43** (4), pp 642–58

Georges, L and Eggert, A (2003) Key account managers' role within the value creation process of collaborative relationships, *Journal of Business to Business Marketing*, **10** (4), pp 1–22

Gosselin, DP and Bauwen, GA (2006) Strategic account management: customer value creation through customer alignment, *Journal of Business & Industrial Marketing*, **21** (6), pp 376–85

Gosselin, D and Heene, A (2003) A competence-based analysis of account management: implications for a customer-focused organization, *Journal of Selling & Major Account Management*, **5** (1), pp 11–31

Gounaris, S and Tzempelikos, N (2013) Key account management orientation and its implications: a conceptual and empirical examination, *Journal of Business to Business Marketing*, **20** (1), pp 33–50

Gounaris, S and Tzempelikos, N (2014) Relational key account management: building key account management effectiveness through structural reformations and relationship management skills, *Industrial Marketing Management*, **43** (7), pp 1110–23

Guenzi, P, Georges, L and Pardo, C (2009) The impact of strategic account managers' behaviors on relational outcomes: an empirical study, *Industrial Marketing Management*, **38** (3), pp 300-11

Guenzi, P, Pardo, C and Georges, L (2007) Relational selling strategy and key account managers' relational behaviors: an exploratory study, *Industrial Marketing Management*, **36** (1), pp 121–33

Guenzi, P and Storbacka, K (2015) The organizational implications of implementing key account management: a case-based examination, *Industrial Marketing Management*, **45**, pp 84–97

Guesalaga, R (2014) Top management involvement with key accounts: the concept, its dimensions, and strategic outcomes, *Industrial Marketing Management*, **43** (7), pp 1146–56

Harvey, M, Myers, MB and Novicevic, MM (2003) The managerial issues associated with global account management: a relational contract perspective, *Journal of Management Development*, **22** (2), pp 103–29

Harvey, MG, Novicevic, MM, Hench, T and Myers, M (2003) Global account management: a supply-side managerial view, *Industrial Marketing Management*, **32** (7), pp 563–71

Henneberg, SC, Pardo, C, Mouzas, S and Naudé, P (2009) Value dimensions and relationship postures in dyadic 'key relationship programmes', *Journal of Marketing Management*, **25** (5–6), pp 535–50

Hollensen, S (2006) Global account management (GAM): two case studies illustrating the organizational set-up, *Marketing Management Journal*, **16** (1), pp 245–50

Homburg, C, Workman Jr, JP and Jensen, O (2002) A configurational perspective on key account management, *Journal of Marketing*, **66** (2), pp 38–60

Ivens, BS and Pardo, C (2007) Are key account relationships different? Empirical results on supplier strategies and customer reactions, *Industrial Marketing Management*, **36** (4), pp 470–82

Ivens, BS and Pardo, C (2008) Key-account-management in business markets: an empirical test of common assumptions, *Journal of Business & Industrial Marketing*, **23** (5), pp 301–10

Jean, R-J, Sinkovics, RR, Kim, D and Lew, YK (2014) Drivers and performance implications of international key account management capability, *International Business Review*, **24** (4), pp 543–55

Jones, E, Dixon, AL, Chonko, LB and Cannon, JP (2005) Key accounts and team selling: a review, framework, and research agenda, *Journal of Personal Selling & Sales Management*, **25** (2), pp 181–98

Jones, E, Richards, KA, Halstead, D and Fu, FQ (2009) Developing a strategic framework of key account performance, *Journal of Strategic Marketing*, **17** (3–4), pp 221–35

Lacoste, S (2016) Perspectives on social media ant its use by key account managers, *Industrial Marketing Management*, **54**, pp 33–43

Marcos-Cuevas, J, Nätti, S, Palo, T and Ryals, LJ (2014) Implementing key account management: intraorganizational practices and associated dilemmas, *Industrial Marketing Management*, **43** (7), pp 1216–24

McDonald, M, Millman, T and Rogers, B (1997) Key account management: theory, practice and challenges, *Journal of Marketing Management*, **13** (8), pp 737–57

Montgomery, DB and Yip, GS (2000) The challenge of global customer management, *Marketing Management*, **9** (4), pp 22–29

Nätti, S, Halinen, A and Hanttu, N (2006) Customer knowledge transfer and key account management in professional service organizations, *International Journal of Service Industry Management*, **17** (4), pp 304–19

Nätti, S and Palo, T (2012) Key account management in business-to-business expert organisations: an exploratory study on the implementation process, *Service Industries Journal*, **32** (11), pp 1837–52

Nätti, S, Rahkolin, S and Saraniemi, S (2014) Crisis communication in key account relationships, *Corporate Communications: An international journal*, **19** (3), pp 234–46

Ojasalo, J (2001) Key account management at company and individual levels in business-to-business relationships, *Journal of Business & Industrial Marketing*, **16** (3), pp 199–220

Ojasalo, J (2002) Key account management in information-intensive services, *Journal of Retailing & Consumer Services*, **9** (5), pp 269–76

Pardo, C, Henneberg, SC, Mouzas, S and Naudè, P (2006) Unpicking the meaning of value in key account management, *European Journal of Marketing*, **40** (11/12), 1360–74

Piercy, N and Lane, N (2006) The underlying vulnerabilities in key account management strategies, *European Management Journal*, **24** (2), pp 151–62

Pressey, AD, Gilchrist, AJ and Lenney, P (2014) Sales and marketing resistance to key account management implementation: an ethnographic investigation, *Industrial Marketing Management*, **43** (7), pp 1157–71

Richards, KA and Jones, E (2009) Key account management: adding elements of account fit to an integrative theoretical framework, *Journal of Personal Selling & Sales Management*, **29** (4), pp 305–20

Ryals, L (2006) Profitable relationships with key customers: how suppliers manage pricing and customer risk, *Journal of Strategic Marketing*, **14** (2), pp 101–13

Ryals, LJ and Davies, IA (2013) Where's the strategic intent in key account relationships? *Journal of Business & Industrial Marketing*, **28** (2), pp 111–24

Ryals, LJ and Holt, S (2007) Creating and capturing value in KAM relationships, *Journal of Strategic Marketing*, **15** (5), pp 403–20

Ryals, LJ and Rogers, B (2006) Holding up the mirror: the impact of strategic procurement practices on account management, *Business Horizons*, **49** (1), pp 41–50

Ryals, L and Rogers, B (2007) Key account planning: benefits, barriers and best practice, *Journal of Strategic Marketing*, **15** (2–3), pp 209–22

Salojärvi, H and Saarenketo, S (2013) The effect of teams on customer knowledge processing, *esprit de corps* and account performance in international key account management, *European Journal of Marketing*, **47** (5/6), pp 987–1005

Salojärvi, H, Sainio, LM and Tarkiainen, A (2010) Organizational factors enhancing customer knowledge utilization in the management of key account relationships, *Industrial Marketing Management*, **39** (8), pp 1395–402

Sharma, A (2006) Success factors in key accounts, *Journal of Business & Industrial Marketing*, **21** (3), pp 141–50

Sharma, A and Evanschitzky, H (2016) Returns on key accounts: do the results justify the expenditures?, *Journal of Business & Industrial Marketing*, **31** (2), pp 174–82

Shi, LH, White, JC, McNally, RC, Tamer Cavusgil, S and Zou, S (2005) Executive insights: global account management capability: insights from leading suppliers, *Journal of International Marketing*, **13** (2), pp 93–113

Shi, LH, White, JC, Zou, S and Cavusgil, ST (2010) Global account management strategies: drivers and outcomes, *Journal of International Business Studies*, **41** (4), pp 620–38

Shi, LH and Wu, F (2011) Dealing with market dynamism: the role of reconfiguration in global account management, *Management International Review*, **51** (5), pp 635–63

Storbacka, K (2012) Strategic account management programs: alignment of design elements and management practices, *Journal of Business & Industrial Marketing*, **27** (4), pp 259–74

Sullivan, UY, Peterson, RM and Krishnan, V (2012) Value creation and firm sales performance: the mediating roles of strategic account management and relationship perception, *Industrial Marketing Management*, **41** (1), pp 166–73

Swoboda, B, Schlüter, A, Olejnik, PCE and Morschett, D (2012) Does centralising global account management activities in response to international retailers pay off? *Management International Review*, **52** (5), pp 727–56

Toulan, O, Birkinshaw, J and Arnold, D (2006) The role of interorganizational fit in global account management, *International Studies of Management & Organization*, **36** (4), pp 61–81

Tzempelikos, N and Gounaris, S (2013) Approaching key account management from a long-term perspective, *Journal of Strategic Marketing*, **21** (2), pp 179–98

Tzempelikos, N and Gounaris, S (2015) Linking key account management practices to performance outcomes, *Industrial Marketing Management*, **45**, pp 22–34

Vanharanta, MJP, Gilchrist, AD, Pressey, A and Lenney, P (2014) The reflexive turn in key account management: beyond formal and post-bureaucratic prescriptions, *European Journal of Marketing*, 48 (11/12), pp 2071–104

Wagner, ER and Hansen, EN (2004) A method for identifying and assessing key customer group needs, *Industrial Marketing Management*, 33 (7), pp 643–55

Wengler, S (2007) The appropriateness of the key account management organization, *Journal of Business Market Management*, 1 (4), pp 253–72

Wengler, S, Ehret, M and Saab, S (2006) Implementation of key account management: who, why, and how?: an exploratory study on the current implementation of key account management programs, *Industrial Marketing Management*, 35 (1), pp 103–12

Wilson, K and Woodburn, D (2014) The impact of organisational context on the failure of key and strategic account management programmes, *Journal of Business & Industrial Marketing*, 29 (5), pp 353–63

Winter, SG (2003) Understanding dynamic capabilities, *Strategic Management Journal*, 24 (10), pp 991–95

Woodburn, D and Wilson, K (eds) (2014) *Handbook for Strategic Account Management*, John Wiley & Sons Ltd, Chichester

Workman, JP, Homburg, C and Jensen, O (2003) Intraorganizational determinants of key account management effectiveness, *Journal of the Academy of Marketing Science*, 31 (1), pp 3–21

Zupancic, D (2008) Towards an integrated framework of key account management, *Journal of Business & Industrial Marketing*, 23 (5), pp 323–31

Zupancic, D and Müllner, M (2008) International key account management in manufacturing companies: an exploratory approach of situative differentiation, *Journal of Business to Business Marketing*, 15 (4), pp 455–75

INDEX

Note: The index is filed in alphabetical, word-by-word order. Numbers within main headings are filed as spelt out. Acronyms are filed as presented. Page locators in *italics* denote information contained within a Figure or Table.